The Currency Cold War

PERSPECTIVES

Series editor: Diane Coyle

The Currency Cold War

Cash and Cryptography,
Hash Rates and Hegemony

David G. W. Birch

LONDON PUBLISHING PARTNERSHIP

Published by London Publishing Partnership
www.londonpublishingpartnership.co.uk

Published in association with
Enlightenment Economics
www.enlightenmenteconomics.com

ISBN: 978-1-913019-07-5 (hbk)

A catalogue record for this book is
available from the British Library

This book has been composed in Candara

Copy-edited and typeset by
T&T Productions Ltd, London
www.tandtproductions.com

Cover design by James Shannon
www.jshannon.com

Printed and bound by TJ International Ltd,
Padstow, Cornwall

Dedicated to the person who first encouraged me to write a book at all: Diane Coyle. It is because of her that this book went from concept to manuscript in a time I would not have thought possible a few years back!

Contents

Foreword by Michael J. Casey

Money, the Israeli historian Yuval Harari tells us, 'is the most successful story ever invented and told by humans'.

Harari's intent, in reminding us that money is fiction, is not to diminish its significance or warn us against relying on it. On the contrary. As he argues in his seminal book *Sapiens: A Brief History of Humankind* (2011), our unique capacity to tell and collectively believe in stories is the single most important factor behind human dominance of the planet. Some of our most formative stories include those we tell about religion, about companies being 'legal persons', and about nations as communities of shared values. But it is money that is the big one: the story that has contributed most to the build-out of civilization. After all, as Harari observes, 'not everybody believes in God, not everybody believes in human rights, not everybody believes in nationalism, but everybody believes in money'.

Reading and listening to my friend David Birch has helped me understand that this fundamental, millennia-long story of money is also one of periodic change. When viewed over the long arc of history, money's otherwise unbroken narrative is filled with constant twists and turns, of responses to changes in the political order, in culture and, most importantly, in technology.

At the moment, as I sit down to write this foreword amid the tumult of early spring 2020, it is hard not to believe our money story is poised for one of its more dramatic plot shifts. We do not know for sure what direction it will take, but what we can see is a unique convergence of three forces that seem, to me at least, certain to bring about profound change of some sort.

The first is geopolitical. Ever since the financial crisis of 2008, top economic thinkers have been warning that imbalances in the global economy are putting stress on the International Monetary and Financial System.

By some measures, the US dollar's central role in that system – in place since the Bretton Woods Agreement of 1944 – has never been stronger. As reflected in its overwhelming dominance when it comes to total central bank reserves, cross-border payments, foreign exchange trades and, most significantly, international corporate assets and liabilities, the greenback is more powerful than ever. But the world's concentrated dependence on the US dollar is actually the system's core weakness. It means that in moments of crisis, the US Federal Reserve (Fed) feels compelled to act not only as a lender of last resort to US banks, but also – in contradiction to its domestic economic mandate – as the ultimate financial backstop to the entire world. It also means that when the Fed is acting purely within its domestic mandate and adjusts monetary policy to optimize US economic conditions, it unwittingly delivers collateral damage to other countries, setting off waves of 'hot money' flows into and out of foreign currencies with every quarter-point cut or hike in US interest rates. This fosters exchange rate mismatches that fuel risks of a race-to-the-bottom currency war akin to that of the 1930s. In the age of Donald Trump, these tensions have grown more acute as the United States has pursued a more mercantilist, America-first trade policy, and as the president's persistent criticism of the Fed's monetary policy has raised questions about its independence.

The second trend pointing to a monetary paradigm shift is technological in nature. The post-global financial crisis era has also seen an explosion in innovation within the world of money. Spurred by mobile phones and the Internet of Things, artificial intelligence and, most importantly, the invention of cryptocurrencies, blockchains and other forms of decentralized ledger-keeping, a new software 'stack' of monetary and financial protocols and applications is taking shape. Together, its components are forging an extensible, application programming interface-capable platform upon which entrepreneurs and governments will forge an exciting, disruptive and also slightly terrifying new era of programmable money – or, as the author puts it, 'very smart money'.

These first two converging trends have already fuelled debate about whether the solution to the international monetary system's imbalances lies in digital currencies. You will read in the pages ahead, for example, about outgoing Bank of England governor Mark Carney's bold vision for the International Monetary Fund to steward creation of a digitally rendered 'synthetic hegemonic currency' to replace the dollar as the world's reserve unit. But it took a third, massively disruptive societal upheaval – the fallout from the Covid-19 pandemic – to turn this gradual two-trend convergence into something even more powerful and urgent.

The global health crisis of 2020, which quickly also became a financial, economic and political crisis, threatens to redraw the boundaries of economic power – not only across countries, but also within them – as centralized governments' failure to rapidly respond has shone a light on alternative models that embrace decentralized governance. Such political fragmentation will almost certainly give rise to alternative approaches to money. For example, it is surely a moment for community currencies to shine.

This crisis has already given rise to a watershed moment for digital currency policymaking. A digital dollar proposal, something unthinkable in February 2020, made it into a March 2020 Covid-19 response bill proposed by House of Representatives lawmakers. This would have required the Fed to create a direct-to-citizen system of digital accounts. The idea was that ordinary Americans, millions of them facing immediate unemployment, could receive fast-relief financial distributions from the federal government rather than having to rely on the banking system's slow, byzantine and restrictive cheque-distribution process. The half-baked proposal was subsequently removed, but it marked a dramatic widening in the Overton window of what is open to discussion. A digital dollar is now on the table.

Meanwhile, an early-April report from the Bank for International Settlements predicted that concerns over the safety of 'dirty' banknotes would lead central banks to accelerate their various digital currency projects. It is striking, too, that 'social distancing' has moved our human connections even more deeply into an online, digital existence: a trend that lends itself even more to digital money and finance. As nearly everything goes online, questions around the interplay between privacy, cybersecurity, identity and money will demand answers that will also fuel changes in how we transact. By making life almost entirely virtual, we have unwittingly given even greater oversight to big data-aggregating internet giants such as Google and Amazon. As such, I believe public interest will grow in less exploitive peer-to-peer systems for exchanging both money and data.

The stage is set, in other words, for an intense global competition to define the future of money – for a 'currency cold war'. As governments and businesses weigh alternatives to a US-centric monetary system, Washington's digital competitors will come at it from all sides. Challenges loom not only from China, whose Digital Currency/Electronic Payment (DCEP) system is already far ahead of the Fed's digital currency efforts, but also from private offerings such as Libra, a fiat currency-backed digital currency founded by Facebook and two-dozen corporate partners. Initially, governments resisted Libra, throwing regulatory barriers in its way. But crises create strange bedfellows. Libra and its imitators retain significant influence over how this all pans out.

Meanwhile, as governments and companies fight over who gets to define our future fiat-backed currency system, we cannot discount the role of decentralized alternatives such as Bitcoin, even as sideline players. David and I might disagree on this, but I see post-Covid-19 political fragmentation breeding demand for Satoshi Nakamoto's invention, which will represent an alternative – if not a more stable – store of value.

Trust in both governments and corporate gatekeepers will be challenged by Covid-19 politics. Those who bemoan the lack of accountability in unprecedented fiscal and monetary stimulus packages could be very amenable to a new idea of money. For others who fear the surveillance powers of both corporate- and state-issued currencies, the alternative of depoliticized, pro-privacy digital currencies such as Bitcoin will be attractive. Bitcoiners have struggled to come up with a coherent narrative in the 11 years since the cryptocurrency's invention. As of now, the analogy of digital gold is looking very relevant.

In other words, the coming currency cold war will be a blockbuster tale. However it plays out, the story of money will never be the same. We are not talking about a mere plot twist, but a wholesale reimagination of how money interacts with society, including a diminishment of the role played by the banking system, which has dominated monetary creation and distribution since the fifteenth century.

To set you up for such a momentous shift in narrative, I cannot think of a more able storyteller than David Birch. In this unbelievably timely, prescient book, your narrator will walk you through both the high-level economic and social stakes as well as the technical and commercial pros and cons of the different combatants. He will never shy away from his personal view but will, with humility and self-deprecating good humour, also recognize and explain the possibilities posed by the many other alternatives. In doing so, the author achieves something remarkable: he takes a topic of higher importance than almost any other at this time, yet one that many would otherwise find too complex and unwelcoming, and makes it relevant and accessible to everyone.

Money is the story of human civilization. Here is your chance to see where it is headed.

Preface

We need things that draw on the revolution of Bitcoin, but Bitcoin alone is not good enough.

— Bill Gates (2015)

The way money works now is essentially a blip. It is a temporary institutional arrangement, agreed upon in response to specific political, technological and economic circumstances. As these circumstances change, so too must money. Many people think money is about to undergo a pretty significant change as what economists call the 'Bretton Woods II' era of international monetary arrangements comes to an end. This is not just the opinion of wide-eyed technologists obsessed with Bitcoin, by the way. In 2019, Governor of the Bank of England Mark Carney gave a speech in which he said that a form of global digital currency could be 'the answer to the destabilizing dominance of the US dollar in today's global monetary system'. But which digital currency? Will we really be choosing between the Federal Reserve and Microsoft (between dollar bills and Bill's dollars[*])? Between Facebook's Libra and China's Digital Currency/Electronic Payment (DCEP) system? Between spendable special drawing rights (SDRs) and Kardashian kash?

---

[*] I thought of this joke a quarter of a century ago and I never get tired of it.

I think the answer is that these are precisely the kinds of choices we will soon be having to make, so we need to start planning for this coming era of digital currency. The historian Niall Ferguson has written that 'if America is smart, it will wake up and start competing for dominance in digital payments', and I am sure he is right. In fact, I will go further: we could see a new cold war in cyberspace with, to choose some obvious examples, Facebook's private currency facing off against China's public currency facing off against a digital euro. Would a digital dollar win this new space race?

It would be a mistake to see this as merely a technical debate about cryptocurrencies and blockchains, about hash rates and key lengths. It has significance far outside the virtual boundaries of the new age. The dollar's dominance gives America the ability to exert soft power through the International Monetary and Financial System (IMFS). A serious implication of replacing existing monetary arrangements with new infrastructure based on digital currency is that this US power might be constrained. If new currencies prove more attractive to individuals, organizations and governments around the world, America's control over dollar clearing in New York will cease to translate into political power. Who cares about Western sanctions if they are not using dollars or euros, are not sending money via banks and are all but invisible to regulators? Whether you think it might be a good thing or not, you need to think about what it means for you, your business and your country.

It seems to me that, now technologists, business strategists, economists and both national and international regulators are beginning to look in the direction of those alternatives, the whole topic of digital currency needs to be explored. In this book, I will set out its economic and technological imperatives, discuss its potential impact on the IMFS, and highlight its main sources of tension – between old and new, between public and private, and, most importantly, between East and West – in order to contribute to a debate necessary to shape the system of the near future.

By way of conclusion, I will make some positive suggestions about a national digital currency strategy.

Acknowledgements

Many thanks are due to Jeremy Wilson, former vice chairman of corporate banking at Barclays, for his support and advice on my first thoughts on the topic; to Simon Lelieveldt for his constructive suggestions; to Andrew Hilton and Jane Fuller at the CSFI for their helpful comments on a precursor to this work; to the author Jeffrey Robinson for his wise advice on focus; and, of course, to my family for their support during the process of writing this book.

Introduction

I think that the internet is going to be one of the major forces for reducing the role of government. The one thing that's missing, but that will soon be developed, is a reliable e-cash, a method whereby on the internet you can transfer funds from A to B without A knowing B or B knowing A. The way in which I can take a $20 bill, hand it over to you and there's no record of where it came from.

– Milton Friedman (1999)

More than two decades after Milton Friedman's prediction that a 'reliable' digital alternative to notes and coins would revolutionize the new economy, we still do not have such a thing in widespread use. Yes, a few people use cryptocurrencies of one form or another, although mainly for speculative purposes. For most people, however, digital money means a mobile or web front-end grafted to a half-century-old set of payment rails that transport the fiat currencies of the world via laser beams and transistors.

That is not to say the arrival of Bitcoin, in particular, has not reignited interest in constructing alternatives. But what alternatives are there, and why would we want them? It is one thing to say that we should have digital currency, quite another to define it. How would such a thing work? What would we do with it?

Let us remember the starting point. Since the Industrial Revolution, there have been three different kinds of currency, essentially, that have served to support the modern economy.

These are the fiat currencies that we are familiar with today, the free banking currencies that used to exist in many countries (including Scotland) but are now a relic, and the currency boards that still exist in a few places (Hanke and Schuler 1998). It is time to start thinking about the very serious question of whether a digital currency will be either a virtual version of one of these or something entirely new – and, of course, what the impact will be on businesses, governments and societies.

Pyramid scheme

How should we begin to think about the high-level impact of digital currencies? In his 2015 book, *Currency and Power*, Benjamin Cohen set out a 'currency pyramid' as a way of looking at international monetary arrangements (Cohen 2015). I will use a simplified version of this pyramid (see figure 1) to categorize world currencies as one of four groups: the *Prime* currency; the *Patrician* currencies, used for business and by the global elite; the *Plebeian* currencies, which work perfectly well within their own currency areas but are little used beyond; and, finally, the *Permeated* currencies, which exist but are supplanted by other currencies for transactions that matter.

I can illustrate the latter category from personal anecdote: many years ago, I lived in a developing nation where all transactions of any significance were conducted in US dollars and the local currency was used only for day-to-day transactions such as shopping and transport. Anyone accumulating any reasonable amount of the local currency would change it to dollars. Thus, the local economy was *permeated* by dollar transactions.

This pyramid is remarkably stable (as pyramids tend to be, hence their appeal as a visual metaphor) and, as Cohen notes elsewhere, there is no sign whatsoever of an emerging multipolarity in the global currency system. A detailed study of the IMFS found little evidence of competition (Cohen and Benney 2014); indeed, quite the reverse is true. The US dollar is top dog and the euro lags far behind. There are a variety of Patricians (e.g. the British pound), but nothing much has changed for a generation. (The Deutschemark and the French franc together accounted for around a fifth of global reserves, exactly the same proportion as is now accounted for by the euro.)

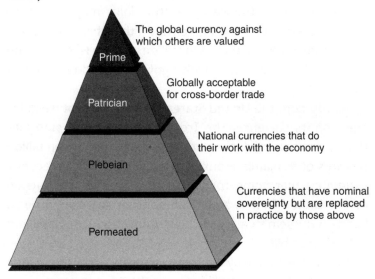

Figure 1. The currency pyramid (after Cohen 2015).

That stability is taken for granted. In Cohen's view, no nation wishing to promote or sustain demand for its currency would abuse its exorbitant privilege as much as the United States has done. Actions that the United States might take to avoid the abandonment of the dollar (deficit reduction, export promotion and regulatory reform in the financial sector) seem to be a low priority in the dysfunctional and polarized body politic of a country that does not appear to treat the reputation of the dollar as a key concern (Cohen 2015).

Cohen draws attention to this because the dollar's role as prime currency, as global hegemonic currency, brings (as is well known) substantial benefits to the American economy and substantial support to American foreign policy. The fundamental exorbitant privilege is measurable and substantial. As Robert Kaplan, president of the Federal Reserve Bank of Dallas, said, thinking about cryptocurrency and digital currencies reinforces the view that 'the dollar may not be the world's reserve currency forever, and if that changes, and you tack on 100 basis points to $20 trillion … [that is] $200 billion a year and all of a sudden we've got a tremendous problem' (Keoun 2019).

As top dog, the United States earns significant 'seigniorage ' on its currency. The Treasury prints more $100 bills than dollar bills, and there are now more than seven billion pictures of Benjamin Franklin in circulation. It was recently estimated that some four-fifths of $100 bills are outside of the United States. American soldiers searching one of Saddam Hussein's palaces in 2003 found about $650 million in fresh $100 bills.

Dollars are printed by the Treasury and issued by the Federal Reserve (Fed). The central bank pays the Treasury for the cost of production – about 10 cents a note – and then exchanges the notes at face value for securities that pay interest. The more money the Fed issues, the more interest it earns. Each year, it returns to the Treasury a resulting windfall of billions of dollars in seigniorage payments (Applebaum 2011).

Revenues from selling banknotes to foreigners aside, America – much more importantly – gets to exert both hard and soft power through the IMFS. This power might be seriously constrained were the currency pyramid to collapse.

For this to happen, there needs to be a technology platform that enables the change (described in *Digital Currency*, part 1 of this book) as well as a social, political and economic environment that is conducive to such a change (described in *Drivers for Change*, part 2). My argument is that both the technology platform and the changing environment make a reorganization of our modern, apparently stable currency pyramid not only possible but also overwhelmingly likely. Quite how the pyramid might change and what the impact of that change will be are matters for informed speculation, but one of the more serious and significant sets of outcomes will focus on the competition between old and new, private and public, and Western and Eastern models. This competition is the subject of *The Currency Cold War* (part 3).

No one can know what the outcome of the impending currency cold war will be, but I have some ideas for how to go about formulating national policy on digital currency. I set these out in the Coda.

PART 1
DIGITAL CURRENCY

The US Government stands more to gain from digital currency than anyone else. Ironically, they don't seem to have figured that out yet.

— Erik Townsend, *Beyond Blockchain: The Death of the Dollar and the Rise of Digital Currency* (2018)

A digital currency is a currency that only exists in the virtual world of computers. It has no 'mundane rump', as sterling does. What I mean by this is that most pounds – around 96% of them, in fact – only exist in the virtual world of computers, with just 4% of them clinging to the physical world in pockets and purses and down the backs of sofas throughout the land. If I decided that I did not like pounds and wanted to create a new currency of my own, it would be a bit of a hassle to have to start minting coins, printing notes and persuading McDonalds to add another drawer to their cash registers. In the world of Apple, Angry Birds and Amazon, though, this is not a problem. I can just make up my digital currency and off I go. Although, as the economist Hyman Minsky famously observed, *creating money is easy: getting it accepted is the hard part.*

Why would someone accept new currency, such as my proposed Wessex e-Groats, instead of euros? Convenience, for one thing. Look at private currencies, such as Marks &

Spencer vouchers or Amazon gift certificates, as a pointer. A friend of mine paid at a farmer's market in Surrey using a Marks & Spencer voucher and got change. Although not sterling, they are a form of currency, in Surrey and no doubt in other parts of the United Kingdom. As I spend a fortune on Amazon, I would have no problem taking a tenner's worth of Amazon gift certificates instead of the tenner you owe me down the pub. The revolutionary capabilities of the internet and, in particular, the mobile phone make this not only possible but inevitable. While it may be difficult to imagine popping to the shops with half a dozen kinds of banknote in my back pocket, it is not hard to picture an app on my smartphone managing these different currencies for me and choosing the best one for the purpose at hand.

It is not all about convenience and efficiency though. Some currencies, and Bitcoin is a current example, are really more ideological in nature. The people who champion Bitcoin are only partly concerned with transactions. They are more focused on removing governments' hands from the monetary reins. You do not trust the government to run supermarkets, they might say, so why let it run money? The same goes for those who advocate electronic gold or some kind of world currency based on commodity prices and the like.

Others – myself included – think that the future of money is connected with the future of communities, both physical and online. In fact, I wrote a book about it: *Before Babylon, Beyond Bitcoin*. In places where monetary arrangements collapsed, such as Greece, we have already seen local groups developing their own currencies to replace the misfiring euro. We have also seen early experiments in the United Kingdom (the Brixton pound in London), in Germany (the Chiemgauer in Bavaria) and in many other places, all of which attracted some attention following the global financial crisis (Halton 2019). None of these have yet attained scale, but the new technologies of cryptocurrency lower the bar to entry, which means we can begin to think about new possibilities. For an obvious example, look at London. The economy of the capital is already distinct from that of the rest of the United Kingdom, so that would be a good place to start. If London started its own digital currency and Scotland started its own digital currency, then their utterly distinct economies could be freed from the mutual shackles of national monetary policy.

Insofar as governments (rather than international bond markets) control their monetary policy, you can see the possibility for some form of oversight or governance. But in a world of hundreds if not thousands of digital currencies, it will be the market that sets the values. Right now, we in the United Kingdom use one currency, sterling, for everything. But I suspect our children might find this as outdated as the Edwardian gold standard I so fondly remember by the nickname 'half a dollar', slang for the half-crown coin of my own childhood. They might use London pounds or World of Warcraft gold when they go shopping but amass Kilowatt cash and Mobility moolah in their pension funds.

So, we are going to see a new world of choice between digital currencies that embody different values, and that is a good thing. This is why it is time to take a look at what digital currencies are and how they might work.

Chapter 1

What is digital currency?

> The history of digital cash can also show us a particularly vivid example of the use of money and technologies to tell us stories about the future.
>
> — Finn Brunton, *Digital Cash* (2019)

So, what is digital currency? It is a kind of digital money that has become a unit of account as well as a store of value and a medium of exchange. So far, so good. But wait: what is digital money? It is a kind of electronic money (e-money) that can serve as a store of value and can be analogue or digital;* either way, it lives inside chips and computers, not pockets and purses.

Digital money, then, is e-money. When people talk about digital currency, though, they generally mean something more than a form of e-money. After all, we already have e-money, and lots of it. In developed markets, almost all money is electronic, with only a small fraction being made up of notes and coins. When people talk about digital currency, what they are really talking about is going all the way and replacing those notes and coins. It is not simply a matter of

---

* We are not interested in the analogue kind, although it did exist. If you are curious about whether analogue computers were ever used in finance, take a look at MONIAC. This was the Monetary National Income Analogue Computer used in 1949 to model the national economic processes of the United Kingdom, and it used fluids to represent amounts of money!

replacing the store of value, either, but of replacing cash as a medium of exchange.

From the earliest days of the internet, people have wanted the kind of electronic cash (e-cash) that would replace physical cash. Here, for example, are Daniel Lynch (a founder of CyberCash, one of the earliest enterprises in this space) and Leslie Lundquist writing in the early days of the web (Lynch and Lundquist 1996):

> What is digital money? Digital money is an electronic replacement for cash. It is storeable, transferable and unforgeable. It is the cuneiform of a new age. As it is written on the DigiCash home page, digital money is 'numbers that are money'.

I rather liked their use of cuneiform as a metaphor, because Babylonian writing arose from the need for accounting and recording transactions.

They go on to describe a canonical set of use cases that define what I might label the Silicon Valley Standard (SVS) definition of e-cash:

> Using digital money, lobbyist Alice can transfer money to Senator Bob so that newspaper reporter Eve cannot determine who contributed the funds.

> Bob can deposit Alice's money in his campaign account, even though the bank has no idea who Alice is.

> But if Alice uses the same piece of digital money to bribe two different members of Congress, the bank can detect that. And if Congressman Bob tries to deposit Alice's contribution into two different accounts, the banks can detect that, too.

The idea that anonymity was the key to creating a form of e-cash that was a 'perfect' cash replacement suffused the thinking (including mine) about digital money in those early days. Here are economist Robert Guttman's thoughts on the matter from more than 15 years ago (Guttman 2003):

> People and businesses will use cybercash if they see it as an untraceable money form, much like cash.

In other words, the desired form of e-cash is a perfect tool for crime. I think it is unrealistic to imagine that this standard will be allowed by the authorities, although whether they will be able to do anything about it is another matter – one that we will return to later when we think about what digital money should do for the new economy.

Let us continue with this line of thinking and say that digital money is a form of e-cash. The crucial distinction between e-money and e-cash is that, if I want to pay you for something, I can send e-money to your bank account, but that is it; I cannot use Pingit or Venmo to put money into your pocket, only into an account somewhere. However, e-cash is just like physical cash: if I send it to you, it is yours. You can stick it in the bank if you want to, or you can leave it in your smartphone, your television or your car: it is up to you.

This is the really big distinction between the e-money of the modern age – the debit card in everyone's pocket – and the e-cash of the coming age. Visa and MasterCard, Amex and Discover, Unionpay and all the others have delivered convenient e-money to everyone on Earth (well, everyone on Earth with a bank account, plus some prepaid cards around the edges), and they have been astonishingly good at it. When I get off a plane in Sydney or Samarkand, I expect to be able to

THE CURRENCY COLD WAR

stroll into my hotel and pay with my chip-and-PIN Amex card. But I cannot yet send money to anyone in the world as easily as I can send them a photo (to steal a phrase from Facebook CEO Mark Zuckerberg).

For that, we need the e-cash that we do not yet have. Since the early days of the new internet age (which I date from 1994, the year of the Netscape IPO), the evolutionary tree of e-cash has been growing to the point where digital currency is now not only a possibility but a racing certainty.

The evolutionary e-cash tree

In order to understand how digital money is likely to work, it is worthwhile taking a diversion and looking at the evolutionary tree – not in exhausting detail, but in order to see why I think it will work in a particular way.

Table 1. The digital currency problem.

	THE IDENTITY ISSUE	THE VALUE ISSUE
What is the problem?	How do I know that it is your money?	How do I know that the money is real?
	The **authentication** problem	The **authenticity** problem
How do we solve it?	Smart devices	Smart cryptography

We can simplify this diversion by observing that creating digital money means solving two essential problems, as shown in table 1. If you are going to transfer value to me, I need to know both that the value is yours to give me and that the value is real. In order to answer these questions, we must solve different but related problems.

The evolution of digital currency is the story of new tech-nologies coming along to solve these problems under the pressures of natural selection in the payments marketplace.

The authentication problem

When the internet first came along, authentication meant one thing and one thing only: passwords. The way that you demonstrated you were authorized to do something or other was by authenticating yourself against some virtual identity using a password.

Passwords have limits, though. It takes an awful lot of back-end fraud protection to make a workable payment sys-tem using passwords because they are just so easy to steal, guess or buy. We simply cannot run the population-scale e-cash system necessary to implement digital currency using passwords. We must move on.

If we assume, broadly speaking, that the 'numbers that are money' are secured using modern cryptography, then demonstrating that you have control over those numbers comes down to the straightforward issue of demonstrating that you have control over the cryptographic keys. This is precisely what happens when I use my John Lewis Master-card in Waitrose. The card has a chip in it, and the chip con-tains a cryptographic key used to form digital signatures. By entering the correct PIN, I am, in essence, proving that I am allowed to use that key and hence that I have control over the money that is being transferred from my account at John Lewis Financial Services to a Waitrose account at some bank or other.

So, in a modern context, the problem comes down to prov-ing you have the ownership of a cryptographic key. You do this every day when you wave your iPhone over a reader to get on the bus, punch in your PIN after inserting your bank card into a shop terminal, or type in your verification code (printed on the back of your credit card) when buying something online. Each of these works with a different degree of security. Having access to the iPhone, remembering your PIN, possessing the bank card, having the correct fingerprint and knowing your three-digit code are all examples of authentication 'factors'. Generally speaking, we are happy with counterparties demonstrating one factor for small transactions, two for medium-sized transactions and three or more for larger transactions.

I should say that, for the purposes of this book, I take the authentication problem as solved and do not intend to dwell on it further. While authentication is a bit of a pain in the backside right now, it will not be for much longer. I can illustrate why using a recent example.

I called my bank to enquire about a new service: not to order anything, just to ask a question about business bank accounts. Now, as is normal when you phone a bank that you have been with for many years, they asked me to authenticate myself using a selection of publicly available information (e.g. my date of birth and my mother's maiden name). They then asked me a series of questions to which they already knew the answers that I had forgotten. In this case, they also asked me something to do with the countries I had been working in recently. There was no way I could remember all of the countries I had worked in over the last few months, and anyway, why should I? The bank already knew, since my phone and all the financial apps I use all the time were in those countries with me.

You can see where I am going with this. These financial apps not only know who I am and where I am, but also what I have been doing. They know everything about me, yet they do not seem able to do much with this data. But they should be! The combination of bank and mobile operator really ought to deliver something special. For example, the end of PINs and passwords should come about because of continuous passive authentication: software running in my smartphone that checks how I hold the phone, where I go, what I do, how I type and so on. That way, next time the bank calls, there will be no questions about my mother's maiden name or my PIN because the phone should already know whether it is me or not.

The launch of services such as 'Sign in with Apple' will accelerate the (very beneficial) trend towards strong local authentication of cryptographic keys stored in tamper-resistant hardware. The keys will not be in a chip on your bank card, as they are now, but in a chip on your phone. So, when you tell your phone 'Siri, send 10 Wessex e-Groats to Dave Birch', there will be an auditable record that you, the owner of said groats, gave permission to transfer them to me.

The authenticity problem

If you give me a bank note, I need to know it is not counterfeit. If you give me a digital bank note, I need to know it is not counterfeit and that you have not already given it to someone else. This is an easy problem to solve in the physical world but not in the digital one. Yet it must be solved, because moving from a form of digital money that is held in the accounts of financial institutions to a digital currency that can be held, well, anywhere means moving from e-money to e-cash. As has been understood from the very earliest days of e-money, the crucial problem in the world of e-cash is double-spending. This is the crux of the matter and the architectural foundation of e-cash schemes.

First, counterfeiting: this is an obvious and fundamental threat to any currency, which is why it has attracted such drastic punishments historically. When money in the form of copper 'cash' first appeared in China in the first century CE, the punishment for making fake coins was to have your face tattooed.* By the seventh century CE, the punishment was death for you, your family and your neighbours (Cooley 2008). Had the Tang dynasty offered election pledges, one of them might have been 'tough on counterfeiting, tough on the causes of counterfeiting'.

So, how can I stop you from making up fraudulent e-cash or giving the same e-cash to more than one person? Cryptography actually works quite well with regard to counterfeit prevention and detection, because it is to all intents and purposes impossible to forge a digital signature. (I do not want to digress into how digital signatures work, but take it from me, they do.) Thus, in the world of digital money, this is a simple problem to solve.

Double-spending, however, is a tougher nut to crack. When it comes down to it, there are only two ways to prevent double-spending: online, by having some sort of database to prevent unauthorized copying of value; or offline, by storing value in tamper-resistant hardware where it cannot be copied.

In the beginning, e-cash users had databases. Unfortunately, these have one obvious disadvantage if you are trying to implement the SVS e-cash of the day: no privacy, because the database operator can always see exactly what is going on. As we will see later, though, cryptography can deliver some counter-intuitive services, and it was one of the

---

* I think they should bring this back, actually: if convicted of forging £50 notes, you should have 'there's only one Bank of England' emblazoned on your forehead.

pioneers of e-cash who discovered how to use cryptography in such a way as to have a centralized database *and* provide privacy to users. This was David Chaum, founder of DigiCash.

DiGiCASH

David Chaum launched DigiCash in Amsterdam back in 1990 with a contract from the Dutch government to build and test technology to support anonymous highway toll payments (Levy 1994). Chaum came up with something called 'blinding' (along with a number of other inventions in the field). What this means is that someone issuing e-cash (e.g. a bank) can use cryptography to know with absolute certainty that this e-cash is real but find it cryptographically impossible to know where and to whom it was issued.

Enter the internet. It seemed DigiCash's eCash, as the product was then called, would work very well in this new online environment, delivering the anonymity of cash into a digital space. A few banks signed up to experiment with the new system, but it never gained any traction; DigiCash eventually filed for bankruptcy in 1998. It turned out that consumers were not interested in anonymity and were wholly content to use their credit cards to buy things online. If you had to get an account at a bank to use e-cash, they reasoned, then you might as well use the credit card the bank gave you.

Of course, if you do not know to whom a sum of e-cash was issued, then you have to guard against double-spending even more. DigiCash did this by maintaining a database of used coins. Thus, if someone sent you some e-cash, you could check the database to make sure it had not already been spent.

DigiCash was a valuable experiment: an attempt to use PCs and the internet to create an alternative payment network centred on the individual. It contained many ideas that were influential in later developments in cryptography, but it was just as important, I think, in delivering lessons about

> how to get an entirely new, online form of money to work (or not).

Around the same time that DigiCash was launched, NatWest in the United Kingdom decided to try a really radical experiment with digital money by creating a scheme that allowed true person-to-person value transfer: a genuine attempt to deliver e-cash into the mass market. Rather than a database, however, they decided to use hardware to prevent double-spending.

MONDEX

Mondex was invented by Tim Jones and Graham Higgins at the National Westminster Bank (NatWest) in 1990. Although pilot schemes were launched around the world, Mondex never took off, with limitations in both technology and business model preventing it from 'crossing the chasm'. For example, it was a pain to get hold of. I can remember the first time I walked into the bank to get a card. I wandered in with £50 and expected to wander out with that £50 loaded onto a card, but it did not work like that. I had to set up an account and fill out some forms and then wait for the card to be posted to me. Most people could not be bothered to do any of this, so only around 14,000 cards were ever actually issued.

When you eventually got a card, you had to go to an ATM to load money onto it. The banks involved in the project chose an especially crazy way to implement the ATM interface. Remember, you had to have a bank account to get one of these cards, and that meant you also had an ATM card. If you wanted to load money onto your Mondex card, you had to go to the ATM with your ATM card, put your ATM card into the machine, enter your PIN and then select 'Mondex value' or whatever the menu said. Only then could you put

> your Mondex card into the machine. Most people never bothered. If you go to an ATM with your ATM card, then you might as well get cash, which is what people did.

There were a variety of other smart card-based schemes around at the time (e.g. Visa Cash), but these were account based and did not facilitate direct card-to-card (or device-to-device) transmission of value. Meanwhile, DigiCash was not the only database-based software e-cash experiment of the time: far from it. There were experiments in creating 'coins' using different types of cryptography, such as DEC's Millicent, QPass and eCharge (Essex 1999), as well as experiments in using different forms of value (e.g. e-gold, Beenz, Flooz and so on).

There was a lot of creativity, but nothing could beat the banks and their incumbent payment systems. Even banks found it difficult to move from e-money to e-cash. And this was not only in America: there was a burgeoning family of software e-cash solutions being explored around the world. An early example was CyberCoin – or BarclayCoin, as it was known in the United Kingdom.

BARCLAYCOIN

I took Milton Friedman's demand for cash for the internet seriously from the very beginning, and I was sure there would be others with the same demand. In 1997, I took part in a basic experiment with paid internet content (Birch 1998). For this experiment, my colleagues and I chose the Barclays BarclayCoin scheme, which was based on the CyberCoin scheme developed by the US internet-payment pioneers CyberCash. This was a software-based scheme that required consumers to download a free wallet onto their computer. The wallet was then charged up (using a credit card) to hold digital money that could be spent on the web. It was free to download from Barclays.

Once a customer had the wallet, they could go online and start buying. When they clicked on a link to the digital product they wanted to buy, they were sent an encrypted version of the product that triggered the wallet to ask them to confirm the payment. If the customer confirmed, the balance in their wallet was reduced and the merchant's account was credited. Then, the key for decrypting the product was made available to the customer's wallet, and the product could be used. As consumers spent money, it accumulated in the merchant's BarclayCoin account (less Barclays' commission, which was 25%). This charge may seem high, but it was typical for micropayment schemes involving digital goods. Indeed, it is approximately the same as Apple's present-day commission of 30% on sales made through its app store.

In our experiment, we decided to sell 'unlocked' versions of the most popular papers downloaded from the library section of our website, to see if clients were prepared to pay to download more useful versions of the documents they could get for free. And they were. Our experience over the months of this pilot suggested that around 7% of the people who downloaded papers were willing to pay for more accessible unlocked versions. In addition, more people would have made a purchase if they had possessed an agreeable means of payment: a very high proportion of those downloading the free unlocked versions of the documents followed the link to purchase (for £1–£2.50) unlocked versions of the same documents. (At which point they gave up, because they could not be bothered to find out what BarclayCoin was or install it.)

In time, content providers developed attractive subscription-based models that consumers, at least during the first phase of internet evolution, found much easier to understand and navigate. I do not want to reopen the e-cash micropayment debate here, but, personally, I do feel the subscription-based business model might be peaking. I also agree with the noted venture capitalist Fred Wilson, who wrote in his review of the last decade that 'a subscription overload backlash is emerging as many consumers have signed up for more subscriptions than they need and in some cases can afford' (Wilson 2019). My subscriptions to Netflix, Amazon Prime, Sky Sports and *The Economist* – my subscription to *this* and my subscription *that* – are starting to add up to a pretty penny. So, maybe it *is* time to revisit that e-cash micropayment model (once we get over Bitcoin's usability issues and find ourselves with more user-friendly digital options, of course).

The combination of technological limitations and the rise of subscription-based business models meant none of these first attempts to create something truly new went anywhere. The cryptographic solutions were too complex, the commercial solutions did not support person-to-person transfers (who remembers the Secure Electronic Transactions, or SET, standard?), and web browsers did not support encryption or authentication anyway (Green 2018). It looked as if no person-to-person solution would gain traction.

Then along came PayPal.

PayPal

The company was established in 1998 (under the name Confinity) to develop security software for hand-held devices such as the PalmPilot. PayPal itself was a money-transfer service developed within Confinity and, as *The Economist* observed at the time, was 'more like real digital money, because it allow[ed] consumers to pay each other as well as merchants' (*Economist* 2000).

THE CURRENCY COLD WAR

As an aside, I must note that there were plenty of email payment services springing up around that time too. Does anyone remember Citibank's c2it service, which was shuttered in 2003, or Yahoo!'s PayDirect, which launched at the same time?* Or, indeed, eBay's Billpoint service?

In 2000, Confinity merged with Elon Musk's online banking start-up X.com, which soon terminated other operations to focus on its money-transfer business. The company, at that point renamed PayPal, went public in 2002 and was soon acquired by eBay (at a time when around a quarter of eBay auctions were paid for via PayPal).

In 2005, by which time 1 in 10 British people had a PayPal account, the company acquired VeriSign. It continued to grow and evolve its services so successfully that after its first decade PayPal had 100 million users in 25 countries.

In 2011, PayPal acquired the mobile payment player Zong (led by David Marcus, of whom more later) before adding Braintree and Venmo to its arsenal in 2013, further strengthening its position with consumers and merchants.

In 2015, PayPal was spun out of eBay and acquired the digital money-transfer company Xoom in order to strengthen its business internationally. It went on to buy the Swedish mobile acquirer iZettle for a couple of billion dollars in 2018 (PayPal's largest acquisition to date), and, at the time of writing, is generating group revenues above four billion dollars per quarter, as shown in figure 2.

PayPal is an astonishing success story, becoming part of the financial landscape relatively quickly. With its acquisitions of Braintree and Venmo in particular, it became integral to the financial lives of Americans. In one sense, though, it does not represent a revolution: underneath its facade of convenience, everything is running on old rails.

---

* See 'Citigroup to drop its online P2P payments service' (*American Banker* 2003) and 'Yahoo! offers buyers and sellers person-to-person payment option' (*E-Commerce in Finance* 2000).

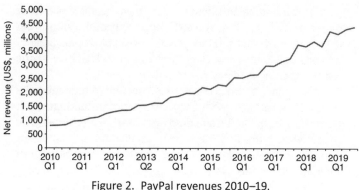

Figure 2. PayPal revenues 2010–19.

The failure of genuine alternatives such as DigiCash and the continued growth and development of international card schemes and domestic payment networks meant that, in the mid-2000s, some observers were questioning whether an alternative to bank-led payment infrastructures would ever get off the ground.

This perspective changed with the arrival of M-Pesa.

M-PESA

M-Pesa is so important that its origins and trajectory need to be recorded and reported from many perspectives. Back in 2003, Safaricom was the market-leading mobile operator in Kenya, with just over half the market. The company had the idea of using mobile phones to make the distribution of loans in Africa more efficient, so it submitted a proposal to the UK Department for International Development (DFID) for matching funding. This was granted, and M-Pesa was born. The pilot launched in 2005, and within a year the scheme had two million subscribers and was handling $1.5 million per day. It was apparent from the beginning that the market was using the product in ways that had not been part of the original business model. In particular, businesses began to use it. They started depositing cash (employing it as a kind of 'night safe') as well as settling transactions and paying wages via M-Pesa. Soon, hundreds of businesses were accepting it as payment.

In summary, a non-bank payment system founded on new technology rather than legacy infrastructure had changed people's lives in ways that could not have been envisaged by those who created it. The scheme, which allows people to deposit and withdraw cash from accounts associated with their mobile phone numbers, has been an incredible success, with more than two-thirds of Kenya's adult population using it and tens of thousands of agents allowing consumers to pay cash into the system or take cash out of it. To put these numbers into context, it took banks in Kenya a century to create a mere 1,000 bank branches, 1,500 ATMs and 100,000 credit card customers.

A key lesson that I took from this project was that a bank-led solution would not have triggered the innovation revolution that M-Pesa did. A key element of its success is that it was born of TELCO culture and conceived as an infrastructure on which others could build. Cashless schools, pay-for-use water, e-health and an incredible range of applications have been made possible by the ready availability of a mass-market payment system for the twenty-first century. This year, there will be some three billion mobile money transactions in Kenya. Not all of them will be sent through M-Pesa, but *almost* all of them will.

Let us recap. Moving from a form of digital money that is held in the accounts of financial institutions to a digital currency that is a form of money which can be held in any number of places means solving the authenticity problem in moving from e-money to e-cash. As has been understood from the earliest days of digital money, the crucial issues in the world of e-cash are the (solved) authentication problem and the (solved) authenticity problem. These are at the crux of the matter and provide the architectural foundation of e-cash schemes.

M-Pesa was e-money that used tamper-resistant hardware to authenticate access to accounts holding the data that represents value. PayPal was e-money that used software and some heavy-duty anti-fraud back-end systems to authenticate access to the data that represents value. DigiCash was e-cash that used software: someone sent value to you, and you could do what you wanted with it. Mondex was e-cash that used tamper-resistant hardware to store the data that represents value and to authenticate access.

However, whether it was Mondex, DigiCash or any other e-cash scheme, such systems needed to have an 'operator'. There was someone in the middle making it all work. But clever software people, building on ideas from all of these schemes and more, were keen to find a system that did not require someone in the middle. They kept running into the same problem, though: how could you solve the authenticity problem without tamper-resistant hardware or a database in the middle?

In 2008, someone came up with a genuinely new way to put together the technologies of digital money: cryptocurrency. This brings us, of course, to Bitcoin. There is no need for an in-depth history of Bitcoin here (for that, I strongly recommend Paul Vigna and Michael Casey's *The Age of Cryptocurrency*), but it is useful to highlight a few points that will be relevant to our discussion about forms of digital currency later on.

BITCOIN

The Bitcoin story is, by now, well known. A person or persons unknown, under the pseudonym Satoshi Nakamoto, published a white paper setting out how to create a person-to-person e-cash system without a central system operator or database (Nakamoto 2008).

At the core of the Bitcoin system were three main concepts: to replace a central database with a shared ledger, to use a new consensus technique to build that ledger absent a central coordinator (this is the 'Nakamoto consensus' that uses 'proof of work' to determine which version of the ledger is correct), and to use a particular kind of mathematical puzzle to incentivize this proof of work. It also did away with the idea of binding cryptographic keys to a value management scheme because ownership of the keys is everything.

The technologies used to implement these concepts were already well known, but Nakamoto had made a crucial breakthrough by combining them in order to embed the incentive mechanism into the consensus-forming process ('mining'), thereby giving an energy to the ecosystem (Brunton 2019).

Maintaining a ledger without any kind of coordinator is a radical way to manage value, and it is wholly understandable why commentators focused on Bitcoin's particular combination of ledger, consensus and incentive (together called a 'blockchain'), which imbued it with a variety of almost magical powers.

At first, Bitcoins were being created as a sort of experiment. But then, in 2010, someone rather famously traded 10,000 of them (now worth tens of millions of dollars) for two pizzas, thus giving them real-world value. Since that time, speculators have made (and lost) fortunes trading ownership of this wholly new kind of digital asset: a digital asset that cannot be copied.

One other aspect of Bitcoin that sowed the seeds for new ways of working was the introduction of programmability. For some observers (e.g. me), the invention of what we might call smart money – that is, money which has its own apps – is actually much more interesting than the peer-to-peer payment system.

The value of Bitcoin, as shown in figure 3, has changed quite unpredictably in its decade of existence, which is why people have begun to talk about creating a different kind of cryptocurrency – a 'stablecoin' – that might be more suited to the mainstream. I do not think this is the cause of Bitcoin's lack of adoption, however. For this, I refer back to the examples of DigiCash, Mondex and the others. Most people simply do not have the problem that Bitcoin solves (which is censorship resistance), and Bitcoin does not solve the problem they do have (which is, broadly speaking, the need for simplicity and reliability).

Whether you think Bitcoin will replace central bank money or not, it is clear that we have now evolved a 'meta-technology' for e-cash as well as (more importantly) a narrative for e-cash that takes it away from institutions and intermediaries. This can be used to create a wholly new form of digital money: cryptocurrency (or, annoyingly, 'crypto').

Digital and crypto

I find much of the conversation around digital currency frustrating. There are frequent commentaries that seem to randomly switch between the terms 'virtual money', 'e-cash', 'cryptocurrency' and 'digital fiat' to the point that they become essentially meaningless. Hence, before we go any further, I think it might be useful to spend some time building a framework that we can use to discuss the topic in a productive way. The crucial role of this framework will be to separate the concepts of digital currency and cryptocurrency. They are related, of course, but they are not the same thing at all.

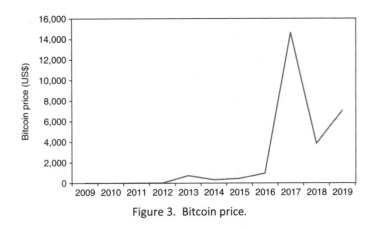

Figure 3. Bitcoin price.

The tree of e-cash has evolved to the point where, in essence, the meta-technology means that anyone can now use cryptocurrency to create their own digital money. It is time to get into the nuances before we look at how we might use the technology of the former to implement the latter. My general view is that we are going to get digital money, but it almost certainly will not be cryptocurrency. However, it almost certainly *will* use the technologies of cryptocurrency, just not as they are used now.

So, let us start with the big question: will a Prime or a Patrician digital currency be a cryptocurrency? The answer is most likely no, but we might use cryptocurrency as a base layer and create a digital currency on top of it, thanks to the magic of tokens (which we shall discuss presently). Kevin Werbach has set out a useful taxonomy, saying that (Werbach 2018)

- there is *cryptocurrency*, i.e. the idea that networks can securely transfer value without central points of control;

- there is *blockchain*, i.e. the idea that networks can collectively reach consensus about information across trust boundaries; and

- there are *cryptoassets*, i.e. the idea that virtual currencies can be 'financialized' into tradable assets.

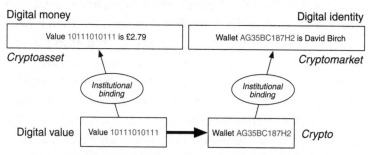

Figure 4. From digital value to real-world markets.

I will use a slightly different, more generalized approach, as shown in figure 4 (because a blockchain is only one kind of shared ledger that could be used to transfer digital values around), but Werbach summarizes the situation exceedingly well. His perspective is that cryptocurrency is a revolutionary concept but that the jury is still out on whether the revolution will succeed. The shared ledger and the assets that might be managed using shared ledgers he views as game-changing innovations but essentially evolutionary. The idea behind such assets, which I will label digital bearer instruments, goes back to those long-ago days of DigiCash and Mondex; however, the idea of implementing them using technology that is (in principle) available to every single person on the planet is wholly new.

Here is my take on the situation. We have a value transfer layer that may or may not be implemented using a blockchain but, however it is constructed, makes for the secure transfer of digital values from one storage area (a 'wallet') to another. We then build a cryptoasset layer on top of that to link the digital values to something in the real world. Note, of course, that this cryptoasset layer could be null and the digital value itself could be the value traded, as in the case of Bitcoin. Either way, we have some form of digital money. We then have a cryptomarket layer to link the wallets to entities in the real world (e.g. people or companies), giving us a digital identity.

In this formulation, the transfer of value is between wallets, and there is no clearing or settlement, so the digital money is a digital bearer instrument (whoever holds the cryptographic key holds the value, whether that value is a dollar, a one-thousandth of the Mona Lisa or gold in a depository somewhere). Digital bearer instruments can be exchanged by what the blockchain fraternity insist on calling 'smart contracts' (I prefer the term 'consensus applications'). The general term for these bearer assets is 'tokens', and it is worth diverting for a moment to explain a little about why so many people see the 'tokenization' of financial services as a likely path for the sector.

So ... crypto

If we follow both the technologies and the narratives of e-cash, we now find ourselves in the world of cryptocurrency. I use the word 'narrative' here in its proper sense, because the history of e-cash is a colourful example of the use of money and technologies to tell stories about the future (Brunton 2019). Each step on the road to e-cash embedded its own social, economic and political vision of the future into the tarmac. It is not inevitable that the technologies discussed here will follow the Bitcoin narrative (a narrative we might best describe as a protest movement – a money Brexit – rather than as a well-rounded vision of the post-Bretton Woods infrastructure), as we will see in the next chapter: *Technology as Catalyst*. This is why we must clearly distinguish between cryptocurrency and other forms of e-cash.

The Bank for International Settlements (BIS) defines cryptocurrencies clearly, describing them as assets whose value is determined by supply and demand, which are similar in concept to commodities such as gold (BIS 2015). However, in contrast to those commodities, cryptocurrencies have no intrinsic value. The BIS goes on to note the key narrative: the use of technology to allow for exchange without trust or intermediaries. However, it also goes on to note that, while there are no traditional intermediaries (e.g. Electronic Money Institutions, or ELMIs, who hold digital money as a liability on their balance sheets), there are instead new kinds of intermediaries that supply technical services along the value chain.

We may do away with the old institutions, the BIS is saying, but we will replace them with new ones. Meet the new boss, as *The Who* say. Well, sing. This has indeed proved to be the case, with attempts to create a blockchain-based alternative financial system (generally known as the decentralized finance or 'DeFi' movement) finding it very difficult to scale (Krupps and Murphy 2019). DeFi start-ups are trying to build an interlocking financial system denominated in cryptocurrencies. They offer a wide array of lending and derivatives products, available globally, peer-to-peer and without any middlemen, but they have their own systemic risks. Their initiatives all rely on the protocols on which they are built, such as Ethereum, which has faced its own problems with scaling (remember CryptoKitties?). They are also tied to the cryptocurrencies that 'fuel' these protocols. If the underlying cryptocurrency layer does not work, the apps on it will also stop working. It is as simple as that.

As we will see in part 3, DeFi could be a building block in a parallel financial system that some countries might find attractive. Iran, for example, has record-high inflation rates, but by using DeFi, Iranians can borrow from global markets at low rates. Leveraging decentralized exchanges could also help some regimes to convert cryptocurrencies to a variety of other currencies through channels that cannot be effectively controlled by outside regulators (Ratna 2020). Having said that, DeFi is a long way from providing that alternative IMFS. The entire outstanding 'market cap' for DeFi at the time of writing is less than half a billion dollars.

Putting the limited scale (and, in fact, the practicality) of DeFi to one side, we now have our evolutionary tree. Having established that cryptocurrency is not an inevitable form of digital currency, we can begin to look at how we will take the next step and create forms of e-cash that might become digital currencies.

Chapter 2

Technology as catalyst

> [Bitcoin] is a remarkable cryptographic achievement ... The ability
> to create something which is not duplicable in the digital world has
> enormous value ... Lots of people will build businesses on top of
> that.
>
> — Eric Schmidt, executive chairman of Google (2013)

Whether Bitcoin is the future of money or not, there is no
doubt it was the release of Satoshi Nakamoto's now-fa-
mous white paper in 2008 which catalyzed the new era of
e-cash that may well lead to digital currencies being put to
mainstream use in the foreseeable future. Schmidt's point is
surely correct: people will build businesses on top of cryptocurrencies. Perhaps some of those businesses will form a new
DeFi system that will overthrow the IMFS and all of its institutions. Perhaps not. Regardless, it is surely the case that a new
and more efficient infrastructure will emerge.

But will advances in technology mean that digital currencies (whether private or public, from central banks or online
communities) will be cryptocurrencies? That is far from clear.
For our purposes, it is sensible to think of cryptocurrency as
a meta-technology for digital currency. It is an arrangement
of technologies that forms, as Schmidt says, a platform for
new products and services. At this point, then, we should
have a more detailed look at the technologies that go into

forming a digital currency platform and the new tools that they give us.

The key technologies

We have our e-cash evolutionary tree, so now let us complete a quick review of the technological building blocks at our disposal. I think there are three key meta-technologies that give us the tools we need to implement digital money. I have labelled them (inaccurately but alliteratively, for marketing purposes) biometrics, blockchains and bots.

Biometrics

It is not much of a prediction to say that biometrics have a key role to play in the future of money. Actually, for most of us, they are already on stage in the present of money. With voices, fingers, faces and goodness knows what other biometrics being used on a day-to-day basis by consumers, I remember being unsurprised to see that around two-thirds of people surveyed in Vocalink's *Attitudes to Payments* research report back in 2015 were already saying they found biometrics appealing. The technology has gone from being a James Bond, sci-fi and scary movie plot device to helping us catch an Uber or access our bank accounts.

This is not for the smartphone generation, the Millennials and Gen Xers; many of the customers who look at their phones to log in every day are older persons, such as myself, who simply cannot remember the hundreds of different passwords needed to function in today's world. What is important here is that I can choose how to log in, in a way that is most convenient for me, and this is why biometrics are marching into the mainstream.

The shift was made clear when Apple brought their Touch ID technology into the marketplace. I can remember the conversations that I had at the time with journalists, clients and friends about the introduction of fingerprint technology on the iPhone. I can summarize these conversations as follows.

> **Person:** Do you know that fingerprints can be faked? I heard about a Japanese guy who did it with jelly babies or something?
>
> **Me:** Yes, I know.
>
> **Person:** Your fingerprints are all over your phone, people could easily steal them.
>
> **Me:** Yes, I know.
>
> **Person:** Criminals might be able to find a way to make a fake finger and use it to buy songs on iTunes using your iPhone.
>
> **Me:** Yes, I know.
>
> **Person:** Do you know that researchers were able to reconstruct useable 3D models of fingers by accessing stored fingerprint templates?
>
> **Me:** Yes, I know.
>
> **Person:** So would you use the new Apple Touch ID on your next iPhone?
>
> **Me:** Of course.

But why is my answer 'of course', given all the supposed security problems highlighted by this fictional interlocutor? Well, it is because Apple Touch ID is not really about security: it is about convenience. Convenience is something at which Apple excels. Before biometrics, when I rode the bus I had to press the home button on my iPhone in order to wake it up, then swipe my finger across its display to get to the unlock screen, then enter a four-digit passcode, then touch my Arriva app to display my ticket to the driver. On my new iPhone, when I press the home button to wake it up, it scans my fingerprint to skip over the swipe and passcode stages. That may not seem like much, but when you are at the front of the queue for the bus, or checking in for a flight, or showing a ticket for an event, or trying to display a loyalty card in a shop using Passbook, it will save you a few valuable seconds.*

Is a fingerprint more secure than a four-digit passcode that can be easily read over someone's shoulder? Yes. Will fingerprints replace four-digit passcodes? No, or at least not on my iPhone. I still have a passcode for the odd occasion when my face cannot be read or when my wife wants to use my iPhone to look up something on IMDB and cannot be bothered to go into the other room to get her smart-phone. Will fingerprints, facial recognition and voice prints make smartphones magically invulnerable and capable of storing your deepest thoughts perpetually and in complete secrecy? No. This is about convenience, remember, not security. Smartphones are not going to be used to launch nuclear missiles (I hope!).

It is amazing how quickly people have gotten used to this sort of convenient authentication. Personally, if I open an app on my iPhone and discover that I have to log in by typing a PIN instead of just looking at the screen, then I am mildly annoyed.

---

* I saw some studies a few years ago for clients in the financial sector at the time that noted there were people who did not lock their phones with a PIN at all, so the arrival of fingerprint scanning automatically improved transaction security for them!

If I am asked to type in a password that I will almost certainly have forgotten, then I am both annoyed and frustrated.

In the early days of smartphone biometric authentication, this is what made me so confident that consumers would like, and use, the technology. I can remember a WorldPay survey of the time (which I cannot find online) saying that half of all shoppers in the United Kingdom were already telling researchers they wanted to use biometrics for payments. At the end of a trial in France run by Natural Security, a French biometric firm, some 94% of users said they wanted to pay for all in-store purchases using fingerprint authentication!

For those of us building digital money systems, there is another reason why using biometrics for authentication in a convenience context provides a much better cost–benefit balance than using biometrics for identification in a security context. This is at the heart of the mass-market proposition, and it is undoubtedly why Apple's decision to add biometrics to the iPhone was such an important step for the industry as a whole. Apple shifted the location of biometrics in the consumer space to convenience, because Apple is all about convenience.

The mobile phone is a safe and secure identity management device: one type of identity it will manage is financial, and one type of financial identity it will manage is payments. This model – convenient local biometric authentication against a revocable secure token in the mobile device, and wireless communication between the mobile device and the local environment – looks very sensible to me.

In order to solve the authentication problem mentioned earlier, we need a marriage of convenience and security that works for the mass market. Fortunately, the combination of mobile phone and biometric authentication gives us this.

Blockchains

Despite being the most widely known use of shared ledger technology, Bitcoin is a very special case. The Bitcoin block-chain is an example of a so-called double-permissionless shared ledger. A double-permissionless ledger, as shown in figure 5 using the 'Birch–Brown–Parulava' classification (Birch *et al*. 2016), is open to everyone to use, and there is no need for any individual or organization to permit or to allow anyone to be a part of the ledger to view, transact in or maintain it.

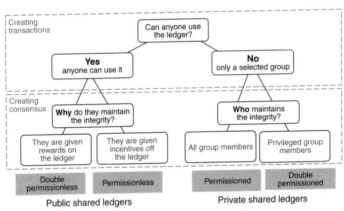

Figure 5. Shared ledger classification.

Bitcoin addresses a very specific problem (a problem that no banks have, incidentally), which might be summarized as 'I do not trust anyone to maintain a truthful copy of the ledger'. The more general shared ledger problem might be categorized as 'I can trust someone to maintain the truthful copy but I do not want them to be able to rewrite history' (Levin and Pannifer 2015). A ledger whose contents cannot be rewritten but which is still reliant on trusted entities to maintain it is one that can be censored. So, as noted, by building a system that does not rely on trusted entities, Nakamoto was able to create a digital asset in Bitcoin that you can own outright and transfer to anybody without permission. Its design follows directly from its objectives. Bitcoin is a replicated, distributed shared ledger designed to enable the existence of a censorship-resistant digital bearer asset. It is, therefore, hardly surprising that bankers and regulators look at it with deep suspicion!*

Having looked at this replicated, distributed shared ledger as a new way to deliver financial market infrastructure – as a new platform for banking that can solve a number of problems – it is natural to ask why market participants do not just pay somebody (e.g. Visa, Vocalink or Google) to run a big database that stores all of their transactions on a big computer, which could run all of the applications under the control of their central authority, which would set the rules. This is a good question, and answering it will take us to this chapter's conclusion, which is that lower costs and higher efficiency may not be the drivers of change.

There are good reasons to think that using this kind of 'hierarchical double-permissioned' ledger will be the choice of the IMFS (Birch *et al.* 2016). Customers can use it, provided their financial institution gives them permission, but *they* are not responsible for maintaining its integrity: banks and regulators are. There are financial technology (fintech) advantages to the reliability, innovation, integrity and flexibility that come from the combination of a shared ledger and shared ledger applications. We are sure that innovators in

---

* However, there is also a good reason why smart observers do not dismiss it: 'censorship-resistant' implies an open, neutral platform that could be a driver of permissionless innovation.

this space will continue to surprise us all, since we are only in the earliest stages of the evolution of a new family of shared ledger technologies.

There are potentially even greater regulatory technology (regtech) advantages. With a shared ledger, banks might not need to declare anything, to anyone, anywhere, as long as their regulators have 'subscribed' to the shared ledger. A permissioned shared ledger could erase the boundaries between compliance and auditing, thus benefiting each party in the bank–regulator relationship. This is not only about sharing access to transactional data, but also about letting regulators have permanent, effortless oversight of more complex automatic procedures as well as execution of agreements. Thus, I am not alone in thinking that regulators are also key stakeholders in the shared ledger-enabled world.

Having described the logic of using a hierarchical double-permissioned shared ledger with regulator-approved applications, precisely which consensus mechanism and shared ledger technology banks should use, which hierarchies they should establish, which kinds of contracts might be allowed (and so on) is, of course, another matter! Let us return to these issues when we design our specific digital money; for now, we will cave to the tyranny of the market and label this layer of digital money infrastructure a 'blockchain', even though the shared ledger used to deliver population-scale digital money almost certainly will not be one.

Bots

It is hardly radical to say that artificial intelligence (AI) will change the financial sector and, therefore, money. It will change the way the IMFS and financial markets work. It is not only technologists who envisage a new future that combines fintech and regtech to create a better financial sector. The Bank of England's Working Paper 274 (published in September 2017), which looked at machine learning in central banks and explored banking supervision, came to similar conclusions. AI is not only a fintech that can help organizations to shift their cost–benefit ratios around products and services, but also a regtech that can help jurisdictions to create better financial services sectors. AI will, in fact, completely reshape financial services.*

What will this mean for digital money? I think it is time for some creative thinking. When financial services people talk about AI today, they tend to think in terms of robo-advisers and chatbots, focusing on the use of AI by their institutions either to cut costs or to deliver new services. Most banking investments in AI are currently investments in machine learning, by and large to target fraud. However, there are other, more radical ways to use AI.†

If you think about it, customers will have access to AI just as powerful as that available to banks. The latter will not have exclusive use of this technology – it will be available on demand to everyone else as well. The smartphones of retail customers and the tablets of fund managers will connect them, permanently, to an intelligence far greater than their own. This cannot happen soon enough for me. I am not smart enough to choose the right credit card, pension or car

---

* John Cryan, while CEO of Deutsche Bank, was famously quoted in the *Financial Times* as saying that his bank would shift from employing people to act like robots to employing robots to act like people.
† As I asked at Digital Jersey's Annual Review in 2018, in an echo of Fred Schwed's 1940s financial services classic … where are the customers' bots?

insurance loan, so clearly I am going to want my bot to take care of those things. But which bot should I pick? The Saga bot? The Virgin Money bot? The best-performing bot in the past 12 months? The Google self-taught super intelligent bot that is also the world Go champion?* While I am not sure I really want to be in the loop when a pension plan or insurance project is being discussed, I do want to be confident that there is a regulator in the loop and that, should push come to shove, my bot will be held accountable for the decisions it has made. Regulated bots are the future, and regulated bots that can exchange digital currencies between themselves are inevitable.

And not just inevitable, but desirable. My regulated bot is going to negotiate with the bots of regulated financial institutions in order to obtain the best product for me. It is not going to be swayed by logos, Google search result positions, branch designs or a double-page spread in the newspaper. It is going to make choices based on price and performance. Thus, if a bank is trying to sell me a mortgage or a credit card, it is wasting its time by showing me gibberish advertisements involving astronauts riding horses, or whatever was in the last one I saw. Brands – the industrial age's mass-market substitute for incomplete information – will become meaningless.

Perhaps regulators will have a list of 'authorized' bots, much as they have lists of authorized financial advisers now. But what if my super-intelligent learning bot outflanks the regulator's super-intelligent learning bot, so the regulator

---

* AlphaGo Zero, which taught itself to play, has already beaten AlphaGo, which was taught to play by humans, by a hundred games to zero. You heard that right: zero.

thinks my bot is acting in my best interests but it is actually acting in Kim Jong-un's or Facebook's best interests? My head hurts.*

How banks' bots will interact with customers' authorized robo-representatives is an unknown that is both fascinating and frightening to contemplate: not for customers, but for banks who may be unable to deliver the cost-effective products and services those representatives will demand. This will be a world where the bank's AI is selling to my AI under the watchful eye of the regulator's AI.

If I am right and AI is an event horizon for the financial services industry, then even though we cannot see (or even imagine) the other side of the introduction of true AI into our businesses, we can see that our traditional 'laws' of cost–benefit analysis, compliance and competition will not hold in that new financial services space. Hence, it is important to start thinking about what the new 'laws' might be and how our financial services can help to formulate them – to step up to the plate of the jurisdictional competition that is certain to emerge.

So, my assumption is that almost all digital money transactions will be between bots and that therefore these transactions can be more complex than those designed for people. This means that we can use the shared ledger applications discussed previously to create not just smart money but *very* smart money.

---

* As the economist Diane Coyle pointed out in a *Financial Times* article (published 26 January 2017), it may be that transparency is the key to making this work, which highlights at least one area where the technology of shared ledgers and machine learning – blockchains and bots – may come together.

Token solutions

We have the meta-technologies we need to build this very smart money. So, let us now think about the architecture of the mass-market digital money that will be built using these technologies, that is, as value that will be exchanged between AIs strongly authenticated by applications running on some form of shared ledger. For this, we need to understand a particular use of the technology platform: the 'token'. This is the final component we require to give literally anybody the ability to deliver their own money into a global market.

Unlike their underlying cryptocurrencies, which have no reality beyond the consensus protocols of shared ledgers, tokens obtain their value by linking to assets in the real world. Tokens took off with the development of the ERC-20 standard back in 2015. ERC-20 defined a way of creating a standard form of token using 'smart contracts' on the Ethereum blockchain. Please note, once again, that smart contracts are not contracts at all because there is no possibility of uncertainty in their execution, and thus no compliance; strictly speaking, they are just automaticity created by the consensus-forming process. The inventor of Ethereum, Vitalik Buterin, says as much: 'I now regret calling the objects in Ethereum "contracts" as you're meant to think of them as arbitrary programs and not smart contracts specifically' (DuPont and Maurer 2015). He later said that 'persistent scripts' might have been a better name, and I agree.

ERC-20 tokens are a kind of fungible value that are exchanged between these persistent scripts: a practical implementation of digital bearer claims on assets with no clearing or settlement involved in their exchange (and, hence, a more efficient marketplace for their trading).*

Picture this: I want to license some IBM software for IBM$100, so I tell my smart contract to send this value to an IBM smart contract. The IBM smart contract then gives me permission to use the software. Using these tokens, it will be possible to implement the programmable money of the future ('this money cannot be used before 1 January 2021' and so on): the smart monies that people have been thinking about for two decades.

When the current craziness has passed and tokens become a regulated but wholly new kind of digital asset – a cross between commercial paper and a loyalty scheme – there will be an opportunity to remake markets in a better way. With reputations depending on an immutable history of participation in transactions, good behaviour will not be gamed and bad behaviour will be on display. Market participants will be able to assess and manage risk, and regulators will be able to look for patterns and connections. I will be able to see that your assets exceed your liabilities without necessarily being able to see what those assets or liabilities are.

With this architecture, we will find ourselves in an era of 'ambient accountability', where the technological architecture necessitates constant verification and validation. This is because of the transparency obtained by using this modern cryptography (e.g. homomorphic encryption and zero-knowledge proofs) in interesting ways. As Salome Parulava and I wrote (Birch and Parulava 2017), these technologies give us the possibility of 'translucent transactions', where

---

* At the time of writing, the trading of tokens has just overtaken the trading of cryptocurrency on the Ethereum blockchain.

THE CURRENCY COLD WAR

the technological architecture means continuous instead of periodic auditing long after trades and exchanges have taken place. We will return to explore this concept in the specific context of digital currencies later on.

One of the first uses of tokens was, indeed, as money. People began to create cryptographic coins of one form or another, and these became known as initial coin offerings (ICOs). Billions of dollars flowed into the first generation of ICOs, a great many of them to Zug in Switzerland (often referred to as Crypto Valley) because the issuers used Swiss Foundation Law to create the tokens. This is why the opinion of the Swiss Financial Market Supervisory Authority (FINMA), is very important. It examined all kinds of tokens, not only ICOs (i.e. securities tokens), and sought to regulate them as appropriate. In its guidelines, FINMA classified tokens into three categories: securities, utilities and payments (FINMA 2018). This was a useful way of looking at them and set the broad outline for how people look at this sector. The US Securities and Exchange Commission (SEC) made a similar distinction, but while SEC Chairman Jay Clayton acknowledged that ICOs 'can be effective ways for entrepreneurs and others to raise funding', he also cautioned that neither payment nor utility tokens have a safe haven if they function as securities.

The worlds of Bitcoins and blockchains, tokens and ICOs come together here in a new architecture for financial services. To recapitulate and emphasize the importance of this architecture, I should point out that once digital identities can exchange digital money with each other in complete security, we will have a functioning base layer for a new financial system built on digital bearer instruments that require no clearing or settlement; this is as opposed to the existing financial system, which is based on electronic currency, accounts and fiat cash.

Such a realistic platform for the digital currency of the future is distinct from the intermediary-free world of the Bitcoin maximalists. As Tim Swanson puts it, the facts on the ground clearly suggest that the vision of 'everyone being their own bank' has no basis in reality (Swanson 2015b). A world of tokens is not a world without middlemen, but it could be a world where the overall total cost of robust and reliable financial intermediation is reduced.

Dumb money versus smart money

As I set out in *Before Babylon, Beyond Bitcoin*, the money created by the communities of the future will be very different from the money of today because it will be smart: money with an application programming interface (API); money that has apps (or 'smart contracts', as some people insist on calling them, even though they are neither); money that has the capacity to facilitate more complex kinds of transactions because it enables so much more information exchange, including a history of the transactions themselves (Rogoff 2016). It is this aspect of the meta-technology that many people find the most interesting. The Association of German Banks, to pick an example, has taken the position that programmable money is an 'innovation with great potential' that could radically alter the way we pay for things and how we store value (Tenner and Utzig 2019).[*]

---

[*] They go on to say, and I strongly agree, that this means it is important to achieve a social consensus on how such smart money should be integrated into the existing financial system.

Smart money knows whether it was held by a sweatshop owner or by a money launderer. It has significant information content. While early experiments with Ethereum and smart contracts, CryptoKitties and stablecoins gave us a sense of the direction of travel, it is hardly wild to speculate that as new technologies connect with these basic building blocks, a new, smarter money will emerge amid the fusion of reputation, authentication, identification, machine learning and AI.

The economist Eric Lonergan has a very optimistic view of where these experiments might take us (Lonergan 2018). He notes that, while in the past different mints and then different banks would fight over issuing money (a competitive environment that may be restored through new technology), it was ultimately Gresham's law that guided evolution. That is, the bad money drove the good money out of the marketplace. In the coming era of smart money, however, it might be the good money that drives the bad money out, as the very same technology used by the Silk Road (the Bitcoin-powered 'dark web' marketplace for drugs and worse) could 'be used to make society more ethical and orderly'. I think Lonergan has a point: the smart money of the future might be smart enough to preclude its use by criminals.

He goes on to say that really smart money would be designed to respond to economic conditions, taking on the key role of smoothing the economic cycle, which is currently in the purview of the central bank. That *is* pretty smart, although to my mind it is only one of the characteristics of smart money that will distinguish it from the dumb money we have today (see table 2). The ecology of the coming currency landscape, instead of being a fiat currency monoculture, will have a rich and diverse set of currencies to help us (well, our bots) navigate the information-rich marketplaces of the new economy.

Table 2. Dumb and smart money.

DUMB MONEY	SMART MONEY
Money that substitutes for memory	Money that has a memory
Standalone money	Money with an API
Money as a value	Money as a distributed application
Money that you can make decisions about	Money that can make decisions about you
Money that is a static creation of the nation state	Money that is the dynamic property of communities

These new perspectives – money as 'local', money as 'translucent', money as 'smart' – integrate to form what seems to me a more plausible narrative about the future of digital money than the libertarianism of Bitcoin maximalists. My assumption is that different communities will choose money that combines different elements. Some might value transparency above all else, while others might want anonymity. Some might desire more sophisticated automation, while others might prize more sophisticated values (e.g. money that cannot be used by outsiders, or can only be used for certain services). Some might want money with a perfect memory of where it has been, while others might prefer money that remembers what is was used for. As an International Monetary Fund (IMF) paper on the subject puts it (see Adrian and Mancini-Griffoli 2019), digital money systems 'could for instance allow users to determine the goods that e-money could purchase – a useful feature for remittances or philanthropic donations'. That is only the tip of the iceberg, to my mind.

An aside: post-quantum cryptography

Much of the discussion about meta-technology here rests on the use of asymmetric cryptography (which uses public and private keys), which is at the heart of the practical implementation of e-money. Before I am deluged with letters from sophisticated and educated readers pointing out that the advent of quantum computing may well render widely deployed asymmetric cryptography null and void ... I know.

In case you are interested in this problem, a National Institute of Standards and Technology (NIST) report on the topic frames it nicely (Chen *et al.* 2016). It notes that in recent years there has been a substantial amount of research on quantum computers, i.e. machines that exploit quantum mechanical phenomena to solve mathematical problems that are either too difficult or too intractable for conventional computers. If a large-scale quantum computer is ever built, it will be able to break many of the public-key cryptosystems currently in use. This would seriously compromise the confidentiality and integrity of digital communications on the internet and elsewhere. The United Kingdom's National Cyber Security Centre (NCSC) concurs that the security of current approaches to asymmetric cryptography, as deployed in real-world systems that usually rely on either the difficulty of factoring integers (RSA) or the calculation of discrete logarithms (elliptic-curve Diffie–Hellman), is compromised by the presence of quantum computers (NIST 2016).

Today, there are two known algorithms that quantum computers can use for cryptanalysis: Shor's algorithm and Grover's algorithm.

Let us start with the former. Attempting to quickly factor large numbers would break both RSA and discrete log-based cryptography. The fastest algorithm for integer factorization is the general number field sieve, which runs in sub-exponential time. However, in 1994, Peter Shor developed a quantum computer algorithm for integer factorization that ran in polynomial time, and therefore would be able to break any RSA or discrete log-based cryptosystem (including those using elliptic curves). This implies that all widely used public key cryptography would be unsecure if someone were to build a quantum computer.

The other algorithm is Grover's, which is able to invert functions in $O(\sqrt{n})$ time. This algorithm would reduce the security of symmetric key cryptography by a root factor, so AES-256 would only offer 128 bits of security. Since increasing the security of a hash function or AES by a factor of two is not very burdensome, Grover's algorithm does not pose a serious threat to symmetric cryptography. Furthermore, none of the pseudorandom number generators suggested for cryptographic use would be affected by the invention of a quantum computer, other than perhaps the $O(\sqrt{n})$ factor incurred by Grover's algorithm.

So, symmetric cryptography as well as forms of asymmetric cryptography built entirely from symmetric primitives, such as hash-based signatures, are not regarded as being vulnerable to quantum computation. This is because the best attacks are considered to be infeasible, provided one uses large enough key (and block) sizes. In particular, when used with 256-bit keys, the AES block cipher is currently considered to be safe from attack by any future conventional or quantum computer.

Vulnerabilities

A summary of the current situation is shown in table 3, which lists the impact of a quantum computer on different cryptographic algorithms, thus highlighting where the vulnerabilities of the latter lie.

Table 3. Impact of quantum computing.

CRYPTOGRAPHY USE CASE	EXAMPLE IN COMMON USE	IMPACT OF QUANTUM COMPUTER
Hashing	SHA2, SHA3	None
Symmetric	AES	Longer key sizes needed
Asymmetric	Factoring (RSA)	Devastating
Asymmetric	Discrete log (DH)	Devastating

To attack asymmetric cryptography, the bad guys would need to perform an active attack (which would require access to a quantum computer) in order to forge a digital signature. However, even without that quantum computer, they could passively collect data now and break key agreements later, once a quantum computer becomes available. This is worth doing in order to obtain the session keys that are used to encrypt message contents in secure messaging systems such as Pretty Good Privacy (PGP). Even if they cannot read any messages now, it is still worth collecting them for when the encryption is broken in future. This means that, according to the NCSC at least, transitioning current systems towards using quantum-safe key agreement schemes should be considered a higher priority than adopting quantum-safe digital signatures.

The timescales are obviously unknown, but bear in mind that even a small 30-qubit universal quantum computer could, in theory, run at the equivalent of a classical computer operating at 10 teraflops (10 trillion flops, or 10^{12}), according to the University of Oxford's Centre for Quantum Computation. NIST's current estimate is that the first cryptographically relevant quantum computer could be built by 2030 at a cost of about one billion US dollars.

Countermeasures

Broadly speaking, there are two very different approaches to protecting against the threat posed by quantum computation. One is quantum key distribution, or QKD. This exploits the quantum properties of physical systems, so it requires specialized hardware. The other is post-quantum cryptography, or PQC, which, as with existing forms of asymmetric cryptography, exploits the intractability of certain mathematical problems, so it can be implemented in hardware or software.

The goal of PQC (also called quantum-resistant cryptography, or QRC) is to develop cryptographic systems that are secure against both quantum and classical computers, and that can interoperate with existing communications protocols and networks. Based on current understanding, the NCSC believes that for most real-world communications systems, and particularly for government systems, PQC will offer much more effective and efficient security mitigations than QKD.

NIST initiated a 'traditional' multi-round process to solicit, evaluate and standardize one or more PQC public-key algorithms. The Round 2 candidates were announced at the beginning of 2019. There are 17 candidate public-key encryption and key-establishment algorithms, together with nine different digital signature algorithms.

These algorithms are, essentially, from three different 'families' that rely on different sources of mathematical difficulty. Lattice cryptosystems are built using geometric structures known as lattices and are represented using matrices. Code-based systems use error-correcting codes, which have been used in information security for decades. Multivariate systems depend on the difficulty of solving a system of quadratic polynomial equations over a finite field. Early opinion sees lattice cryptosystems as both the most actively studied and the most flexible (Buchanan and Woodward 2016). They are capable of key exchanges, digital signatures and far more sophisticated constructions, such as fully homomorphic encryption, which, while not widely used now, might well be at the heart of future business infrastructure in response to the continuing cyberwar around us.

Do not panic

The point of this diversion was to reassure the reader that the problem is understood and in hand. So, when I refer to public-key encryption and digital signatures going forward, please take it as read that I understand that for mass-market deployments in the real world the implementation of quantum-safe algorithms is assumed!

Technology and change

In summary, then, we can say that the meta-technology of digital money gives us a spectrum of options for implementing

digital currency, and that the narrative for that money is probably not the narrative of Bitcoin maximalism. The net result of
all this is that the ability to create digital currency, for good or
ill, has now been distributed and decentralized to the point
where anyone can make money, as we will see in chapter 3.

Chapter 3

Anyone can make money

> [Fiat currency] is another 20th century 'big state ideology' just like socialism.
>
> — Detlev S. Schlichter, *Paper Money Collapse* (2011)

We are used to one particular kind of currency: government currency. The argument for maintaining this monopoly stems from economic efficiency and stability. Society obtains efficiency because a uniform currency with only one issuer minimizes transaction costs in a world of incomplete (or expensive) information. It is not necessary to have information about the creditworthiness of each and every issuer because there is only one. Society obtains stability (we hope) because the currency is issued by a central banker who understands economics (Eichengreen 2019). But things change. Perhaps new technology will mean that information on creditworthiness is no longer an overhead. Perhaps new institutions will mean that stability can rise from new arrangements.

As I said in chapter 2, the meta-technology of digital money has evolved to the point where anyone can now create a digital currency. This observation inevitably leads us to ask the bigger question: who actually will? If anyone can use readily available and standard components to create a digital currency, who might do so, and why might they do

THE CURRENCY COLD WAR

it? I have a '5Cs' framework for thinking about this, which I set out in *Before Babylon, Beyond Bitcoin*. It is reproduced in table 4.

Table 4. Who might make digital currency? The 5Cs.

WHO MIGHT ISSUE MONEY?	WHAT KIND OF MONEY?
Commercial bank *Credit under regulatory control*	Bank money. What we have now, essentially: money is created by banks under central bank supervision
Central bank *National money under political control*	Fiat money. Risk-free money created by the central bank (note that 'risk-free' does not mean what you think it means here)
Cryptography *There is no control beyond mathematics*	Dosh ex machina. There is no issuer and no value beyond the market
Companies *Futures money under commercial regulation; the new world of 'tokens'*	Private money. Currency to be redeemed against corporate assets of some kind
Communities *Reputation money under regulatory control and in a competitive market*	Local money. Bearing in mind that 'local' means something different in the virtual and mundane cases: in the physical world, community is rooted in geography, but in the virtual world we each belong to many communities

Technology is not a barrier to any of these options, to central banks or to anyone else. The idea of a central bank running something like M-Pesa but for citizens is hardly far-fetched. There are tens of millions of M-Pesa users in Kenya, and Facebook can manage well over a couple of billion accounts, so I am sure the Bank of England could download

ANYONE CAN MAKE MONEY

an app from somewhere to run a few million accounts for post-Brexit Britain. There is a middle way, though. The central bank could create the digital currency but distribute it through commercial banks. Those commercial banks would not be able to create money as they do now (only the central bank would be able to do this), but they could use their existing systems to manage it.

If we take the lessons from the success of M-Pesa and PayPal, as well as the failure of DigiCash and Mondex, on board (see chapter 1), then we have a good starting point for the next generation. The latter efforts failed for a number of reasons, but it was primarily due to a lack of acceptance. It is easy to give people cards but hard to give them terminals. It is easy to create e-coins but hard to persuade shops to take them. A decade after Mondex, M-Pesa opted to use neither cards nor terminals; instead, it used mobile phones to vault a non-bank through a regulatory gap to create something that transformed the lives of millions.

Note that both Mondex and M-Pesa used cryptography with hardware at its core to protect the integrity of the system. In the case of Mondex, this was the now-familiar smart card that chip-and-PIN has propelled into every pocket. In the case of M-Pesa, this was the SIM card (which is actually the same thing) that GSMA has propelled into every phone in every pocket. Mondex was decentralized, M-Pesa was centralized; both were managed by a central authority, and in both cases the electronic value in the chips was issued against a 100% reserve in fiat currency held by the banking system.*

_____

* I am sure that when future historians write about the evolution of money, they will say it was mobile phones and not plastic cards that put the final nail in the coffin of cash.

Swedish models

The country where the transition from physical to digital fiat currency is likely to take hold first is Sweden. So, it is sensible to try to understand what the future of digital currency is, and whether digital currencies might fix any actual problems, by looking at what is happening with money there.

Sweden is one of the few countries in the world where the amount of cash 'in circulation' is actually falling. However, as the central bank, the Sveriges Riksbank, said back in 2012, the use of cash is still far too high compared with where it should be on the basis of social costs (because debit cards have the lowest total social costs). At that time, the Riksbank launched a new banknote series, but many Swedes opted to deposit their invalid banknotes rather than swap them for the new cash. The central bank's plan is to drive cash usage down still further, and, as a result, Niklas Arvidsson of the KTH Royal Institute of Technology in Sweden has predicted that paper money and coins will disappear from Sweden around the end of the coming decade (see Foss 2013).

The initial impetus for cash replacement appears to have come from two directions: the declining use of cash in retail outlets because of the proliferation of cards in a highly banked economy, and the introduction of tax changes to make it less attractive to pay workers (plumbers, nannies and the like) in cash to avoid paying tax (Koning 2016). A significant contributing factor to the accelerating decline of cash is that 10 Swedish banks provide Swish: a real-time mobile payment system that transfers money between accounts instantly and for free. Swish was launched by half-a-dozen of the major Swedish banks and, as shown in table 5, is now ubiquitous.

Table 5. The evolution of Swish.

YEAR	MILESTONE
2012	Launched by six Swedish banks
2013	Becomes mobile payment app of the year
2014	Corporate version launched
2015	Reaches three million users
2016	E-commerce version launched
2017	QR codes added
2018	New mobile app launched
2019	48 million transactions per month, 215,000 companies accepting Swish, 7.5 million consumers in a population of 10 million, QR code use rising by one-third each month, 22 billion SEK transferred per month

In Sweden, the anti-cash alliance is a broad church, embracing not only banks and law enforcement but also trade unions and retailers. Not everyone is heading down this path, though. While most of the bank branches in Sweden are now 'cashless' (e.g. 200 of Nordea Bank's 300 branches are cashless and three-quarters of Swedbank's branches no longer handle cash), the slide into cashlessness has caused problems because of the marginalization or exclusion of certain groups. This suggests that cashlessness needs to be planned for; it cannot just happen.

By 2016, polls showed that a third of the Swedish population felt negative about cashlessness. Today, it is around two-thirds (despite almost all of the population having a bank card). A Riksbank review led to a policy decision that the country's six major banks should be required to offer cash services. This was resisted by the banks, because it would increase their costs, and by the competition authority, because it would distort the market by imposing costs only on certain participants.

Nevertheless, the Riksbank has now decided to insist that **all** banks (and credit institutions that offer payment accounts) provide cash services. Given that, as noted, the majority of bank branches do not do so, they will now incur significant costs in having to provide these services again. However, both competition authorities and financial watchdogs are against this revised proposal, and, I must say, I agree with them. The Swedish Financial Supervisory Authority's view is that cash is a collective good that should be provided for by the state (that is, state banks, not private banks, should be subject to the requirement to handle cash). ATM provider Bankomat also argues that cash should be the state's responsibility, since handling notes and coins is such an important – and expensive – part of a country's infrastructure (King 2019).

The e-Krona experiment begins

Back in 2017, the Riksbank began a project looking into the idea of a digital currency: the 'e-Krona' project. The Riksbank itself says that the principal purpose of the e-Krona is to give the general public access to a digital complement to cash, where the state will guarantee the value of the money. At present, the Riksbank (in common with other central banks) only offers its money to banks; all other forms of digital money are private (generally issued by commercial banks). After publishing a couple of reports on the topic, the Riksbank has decided to begin a pilot project to explore a technical solution for the e-Krona in 2020.

While the Riksbank has been explicit that it has not yet taken the decision to issue an e-Krona if the pilot is successful, it is worth noting that, in contrast to many central banks, it is proceeding on the basis that an e-Krona could be a retail digital currency, which, if issued, would grant the general public access to electronic central bank money. This would be a radical departure from the traditional business of central banking around digital currency.

In a recent speech, BIS General Manager Agustín Carstens set out the prevailing alternative 'establishment' view, recommending that the existing 'two tier' payment system be preserved. This, as we will see later on, is the same approach favoured in China.

Cities versus states?

As indicated in table 4, it seems to me that tokens which implement the values of communities (and, because they are 'smart', can enforce them) may come to dominate the transactional space (think of the Islamic e-Dinar or the Wessex e-Groat). While there are many different types of community that might decide to have their own currency, it is the city that interests me most. There are already many experiments underway in our countries' urban centres.

BRISTOL POUND

I could choose any one of a number of examples here, but I will use Bristol to illustrate my point. It is a city in the west of England (and was the 'big city' to me, because I grew up in Swindon, some 40 miles away from this metropolis, and can well remember childhood visits to its attractions). These days, while famous for its excellent university and other cultural attractions, it is famous to me for its contribution to the evolution of next-generation money, being the home of the Bristol pound (B£). Figure 6 shows Bristol pound banknotes (which are lovely, by the way), which are accepted at par at a number of local merchants.

(Just to be clear, those banknotes were issued by a currency board. The Bristol pounds in circulation are backed by a 100% reserve held in another currency. In this case, the other currency is sterling. That sterling is sitting in an account at the credit union.)

Now, while the notes are lovely, they have one distinct feature that sets them apart from the Bank of England's rival product: they carry an expiry date. I think this might be something to do with the law of the land, a crude attempt to maintain the bank's monopoly over currency, rather than an economic calculation to do with hoarding. Nonetheless, it does mean you would be unwise to stuff them under your mattress and forget about them. If you receive a Bristol pound banknote, get out and spend it.

The Bristol pound has been around for a few years. It has made the jump from paper currency to digital currency already, and if you download the B£ app, then you can pay with it at a number of local businesses. Those businesses can also transfer money peer-to-peer within the system to pay their suppliers. However, the trajectory of the scheme illustrates the fate of a great many of these early local currency schemes that come from analogue origins. With some GBP 400,000 of its notes in circulation, the monthly running costs of GBP 13,000 were completely unsustainable. Despite the best intentions of stakeholders, no community can support these costs, which is why advocates worldwide have been re-energized by the possibilities of digital currency.

I am very interested in the world of such city-based currencies and feel quite strongly that their potential is underestimated. Meyer and Hudon (2018) make a useful distinction between 'social commons' and 'commercial commons' as frameworks for new kinds of money. These are frameworks that broadly correspond to the notions of community currency and private currency that I explored in *Before Babylon, Beyond Bitcoin*. The B£ was born in the social commons and was intended to stimulate economic activity within its community.

Figure 6. Bristol pounds.

Earlier in my career, I was more sceptical about this kind of framework and much more interested in the commercial framework. This was because a collection of interlinked community currencies seemed to me less economically efficient in aggregate. I still think this is true, but it may not be the point. I am wondering if we need to explore ways to increase economic activity within communities at the expense of inter-community transaction costs as a response to inequality and the unrest that it may cause. This has several implications, because if communities rather than individuals become central to money creation, then these currencies will be imbued with the values of the communities that create them.

New York, New York

The idea of cities creating currencies that are optimized to meet their requirements rather than those of the nation state may seem far-fetched. But look at the current proposal from New York State Assembly member Ron Kim, Senator Julia Salazar and Cornell law professor Robert Hockett for what has been called a 'public Venmo' for New York. They have proposed a community shared ledger implementation that, if their bill passes (and, it goes without saying, that is a big 'if'), will create a publicly owned payments service and a digital currency that can be exchanged for goods and services within New York state (Hockett 2019b). This is radical not only because it is a financial inclusion play to reach the unbanked and marginalized (who, it is well known, pay a higher price for financial services), but also because it is the first step in returning to an era of currency competition with the nation state itself. Every day, in every way, the future of money looks much more like its past.

PART 2

DRIVERS FOR CHANGE

I don't think a 'cashless society' means a society in which notes and coins are outlawed, just a society in which they are irrelevant.

— David Birch, *Before Babylon, Beyond Bitcoin* (2017)

Technology has created the possibility for change. We have established that pretty much anyone can take advantage of this change and create digital currency.

We have all the components necessary to create private and public digital currencies that could reshape the currency pyramid discussed in the introduction: but why would we? Technical curiosity aside, why exactly would anyone create a new currency, and how exactly would they make a success of it? Early local currency experiments have not gone that well, and the jury is still out on the main supranational fiat currency, the euro. Yet, looking around the world, I can confidently predict that change is in the air: it is no longer just local currency climate change activists or libertarian utopians who are lauding digitalization, but governments, businesses and banks too.

The Bank of England's 2019 review on 'the future of finance' said that the bank should monitor developments in the tokenization of fiat currency to make sure the regulatory, legal and infrastructure implications are understood, and monetary and financial stability are safeguarded. However, the Bank of England saw no compelling case for a central bank digital currency (CBDC) given the uncertainties (Van Steenis 2019). These included legal uncertainties, risks around deploying the technology at scale, unknown effects on monetary transmission and – importantly in the Bank of England's case, where there is a major core system renewal project underway – fear of diverting attention away from improving today's systems.

All of these risks must be studied, but, as we will explore in the next few chapters, the pressure for change is such that they will be overcome.

Chapter 4

What problem will digital currency fix?

The dollar is our currency but your problem.

— John Connally, US treasury secretary,
G10 meeting, Rome (1971)

Of course, when techno-determinist commentators (i.e. me) say that the future of money might be somewhat different from current institutional structures and markets – wrongly assumed to be laws of nature – and that, perhaps, the decentralizing nature of computer communications and cryptography (CCC) means there could be currency issuers other than central banks,* this might be dismissed by scenario planners and strategists as cypherpunk-addled machine-head babble.

The typical, and reasonable, response of most businesspeople when faced with such assertions is to ask 'What problem are you fixing?' To that, I say: my opinion on the current issues with money is, quite frankly, of limited relevance. It is the people who run money who are saying there are problems, not me. There are sensible, knowledgeable and powerful players

---

* As, for example, I did a couple of decades ago (see Birch and McEvoy 1996).

who are starting to talk about radical change in the IMFS. This is why money's stakeholders (i.e. all of us) should take notice of what Christine Lagarde (president of the European Central Bank), Mark Carney (governor of the Bank of England) and others are saying and start to think about the implications of the radical changes that are coming.

The reactions of regulators around the world to one such radical change, the Libra digital currency proposed by Facebook (more on this later), seem to indicate that the incumbents are not going to abandon their positions without a fight. Indeed, the BIS – that most conservative of IMFS institutions – has created a new unit, to be led by former European Central Bank (ECB) executive board member Benoît Cœuré, to explore public alternatives to private digital currency initiatives such as Libra (Kaminska 2019). The unit's first project will be to cooperate with the Swiss National Bank to create a digital currency (using, apparently, some form of shared ledger) for wholesale use between banks.

Cœuré was appointed co-chair (with Jon Cunliffe, deputy governor of the Bank of England and chair of the Committee on Payments and Market Infrastructures) of a CBDC study group set up with the Bank of Canada, the Bank of England, the Bank of Japan, the ECB, the Sveriges Riksbank and the Swiss National Bank, along with the BIS, to assess digital currency use cases, design choices and technology.

Note that this is in parallel to attempts to create a pan-European digital payment service at the retail level, which Cœuré has said is needed to take on US payment strategies and Chinese wallet schemes.*

------

* The Pan-European Payment System Initiative, with its somewhat ironic acronym PEPSI, is currently under discussion, with about 20 banks

What has brought us to this state of affairs? While the prevailing winds were in the direction of change, there is no doubt the storm that blew us here was cryptocurrency. The claims of Bitcoin maximalists to one side, there is definitely something serious happening. Brock Pierce, a noted cryptocurrency investor, was responsible for the first ICO of its kind (MasterCoin) back in 2013, and has invested in a great many companies in the space via Blockchain Capital, the business he co-founded that same year. Pierce is a serial entrepreneur with a track record going back many years. I quoted him in *Before Babylon, Beyond Bitcoin* as saying: 'I think what I've done is the end of all VC, all private equity ... I think all the big VCs are done'.

This may sound ridiculous, especially given the trajectory of that industry. However, there is something in what Pierce is saying. In his book *The Money Trap*, Robert Pringle (a former editor of the well-known revolutionary pamphlet *The Banker*) wrote that globalization has already 'reached the limits compatible with existing international monetary arrangements' (Pringle 2014). There is pressure to change the IMFS, and while I do not think Bitcoin and other cryptocurrencies are the money of the future, they may provide the *platform* for the money of the future. I think I can erect an intellectual scaffolding to support this claim, even if I cannot architect the financial institution of the future that it will be used to build. To Pierce's mind, this would mean a new kind of financial market, because cryptocurrencies have provided the technology to deliver Facebucks (a much better name than Libra, if you ask me), Microsoft moolah and London lollies.

---

involved at the time of writing. This will not be about digital currency but about interoperable push payments.

Proof of crime

Earlier in this book, I talked about SVS e-cash, introducing the idea that a fundamental requirement for e-cash is anonymity. I, for one, thought this in the early days, but I am now less convinced. It seems to me (and others) that the reason there is still so much cash in circulation, in a society where it is vanishing from use in shops, is for purposes of tax evasion, criminal behaviour, money laundering and other undesirable activities.

I do not mean to imply that everyone who wants to keep cash (particularly high-value banknotes) in circulation is doing so purely to help minimize the costs of criminal enterprise and facilitate money laundering on a grand scale. That would be ridiculous. Sometimes, people just prefer cash.

Take Dmitry Zakharchenko, deputy head of the Russian Energy Industry Department of the General Administration of Economic Security and Combating Corruption, for example. When the police visited his apartment, they found $120 million in cash.

Perhaps he did not have time to pop to the bank, or perhaps the night safe was broken. I imagine it must have been rather inconvenient to step over flipping great wodges of cash to get to the bathroom in the middle of the night, so it makes me wonder why he did not either deposit the money in a bank or convert it to something with less volume. Perhaps this is a mass-market use case for Bitcoin after all!

A quick look at the figures coming from the Bitcoin world indicates that while the use of this technology has peaked for 'legit' payments, it continues to climb for 'dodgy' ones. As shown in figure 7, Bitcoin use by criminals grew by two-thirds in the final quarter of 2019 (Popper 2020).

The use of an immutable public ledger to store criminal transactions does not seem like much of a use case to me, but, as the figures show, the underbelly are indeed using it. This was highlighted in the well-publicized ransomware attack on Travelex at the beginning of 2020. This resulted in my bank, Barclays, as well as other high-street banks, including HSBC, Virgin and Tesco Bank, all of which rely on Travelex for their foreign exchange (FX) services, being unable to offer online FX services or process orders for foreign currency for some weeks. Travelex, having left critical security weaknesses unpatched in its Pulse Secure virtual private network (VPN) servers for eight months, was infected with a ransomware virus that encrypted the company's data. The attackers demanded a $6 million payment in Bitcoin to decrypt it.*

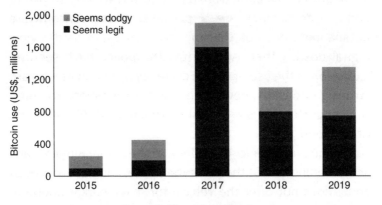

Figure 7. The use of Bitcoin.

The scale of the damage here may have been unusual, but this type of attack is not. Every single day, there is another such story in the media. While we may not care that much

---

* Travelex has not disclosed whether it has paid the ransom.

if finance companies neglect to implement the appropriate security measures and have money stolen, they are not the only institutions being targeted: there are attacks on hospitals and public services all the time as well.

Perhaps we ought to consider following Finland's lead. Back in November 2019, more than 200 Finnish municipalities and public organizations took part in a 'war game' coordinated by the Population Register Centre to practise responding to possible cyberattacks. I am no expert, but I imagine that, among other things, they learned to make sure they had security patches installed on their computers and backups of their data … but I digress.

Let us return to the issue of ransoms. This ransomware would not be much good if the attacker could only be paid in cheques or via bank transfers, which is why ransomware and cryptocurrency are a package. These ransomware datanappers are not the only criminal users of this new digital dosh, either. Apparently, the police have seen an 'explosion in the use of digital currency by criminals who are strolling into cafés, newsagents and corner shops to dump their ill-gotten gains in virtual currency ATMs' (Camber and Greenwood 2017).

We must not panic. If you look at the actual Bitcoin transactions going on out there in cyberspace, it is clear that even crime does not offer the vehicle for mass-market adoption that the more hysterical parts of the media would have us believe. If the demand for Bitcoin were mainly coming from criminal enterprises (and not speculation), then it would actually be worth far less than it is today (*Economist* 2017). There is simply not enough crime. Calculations based on the use of Bitcoin in this sector of the economy put its value at something like one-twentieth of the current price.

I think these kinds of calculations are highly spurious for two main reasons.

First, they are often based on the value of the global market in illegal drugs. While no one can be sure of its exact size, it is undoubtedly a vast market – but a market that is conducted almost entirely in cash. Were these transactions to be converted to digital money, the sums involved would be so enormous that it would be almost impossible for AI machine learning transaction monitoring services to ignore them.

Second, I have yet to see any evidence that criminals are adopting Bitcoin at scale for non-drug criminal schemes. The reason for this is obvious: it is not anonymous enough. A wallet address is a pseudonym, and once this has been linked to a real-life entity in any way, the identities can be connected, monitored, tracked and traced.

Why Bitcoin?

Not anonymous enough? But surely, you are thinking, in the world of Bitcoin, smart criminals can just use 'mixers' and the like to obfuscate the origin of coins and thus confound the authorities. Not likely!

This is because criminals are not using it for large-scale enterprise. As soon as they do, I have no doubt the relevant authorities will take quick and simple action. The currency's lack of fungibility makes it vulnerable to straightforward regulation in that respect.

Whatever Bitcoin is, it is not cash for the inescapable reason that cash is fungible. This matters. Remember that IRS ruling about Bitcoin being a commodity, so that traders would have to track the buying and selling price of each individual Bitcoin in order to assess their tax liability? Here is the salient point (Levitin 2014):

> For a payments geek, the real lesson from the IRS Bitcoin ruling is that for a currency – or any payment system – to work, its units must be completely fungible.

Fungible, from the Latin 'to enjoy', is a great word. One of my favourites, in fact. In this context – money – it means that all tokens are the same and can be substituted for one another. If you owe me £1, it does not matter *which* £1 coin you give me. Any will do. Any £1 coin can be substituted for any other £1 coin, because they are all the same: no one can distinguish one £1 coin from another.

This is not true of Bitcoins. They are all different. And because they are all different, their history can be tracked through the blockchain, this currency's immutable public record of all transactions.

Clever analysts can set their bots scampering along this chain of transactions to find out where money is coming from and where it is going. While Bitcoins may be synonymous with secrecy in the media, we have long understood that blockchain analysis could mean it is surprisingly easy for law enforcement agencies to identify users of this currency (Simonite 2013).*

So, Bitcoins are not fungible (unlike the £50 notes so helpfully provided to our criminal fraternity by the Bank of

---

* If you want a better picture of Bitcoin's role as the supposed currency of crime, a good place to start is 'The 2020 state of crypto crime' (Chainalysis 2020). Chainalysis, co-founded by Jonathan Levin, has sophisticated tools for cybercurrency transaction monitoring and is used by the FBI and its ilk to track down miscreant moolah.

England), which means they can be traced from wallet to wallet. This should make it easier for detectives to get a handle on where any ill-gotten gains are heading.

This lack of fungibility has major implications for criminals. We have just seen the English High Court (in the decision of AA v Persons Unknown & Ors, Re Bitcoin [2019]) determine that cryptoassets such as Bitcoin are considered 'property' and, therefore, are capable of being the subject of a proprietary injunction against a cryptographic exchange (which, in this case, was granted). You can see what is going to happen next: the exchange will be required to identify who owns the stolen coins, and the owner will be the subject of legal action to recover them. This owner might be entirely oblivious as to the origin of the coins, might say they had no idea the Bitcoins they bought were the proceeds of a ransomware attack and might ask to keep them. That, however, is not how property law works. Even if you come to possess stolen property accidentally, a judge can still force you to give it back to the rightful owner.

Smart criminals might use mixers and such trickery to obfuscate the origin of Bitcoins and thus confound law enforcement, but the coins and transactions remain on that public ledger, which anyone can look at. As soon as criminals start using Bitcoins for large-scale enterprise, I do not doubt the relevant authorities will take immediate action, going to the biggest miners in the world and telling them that if they continue to confirm easily identifiable mixing transactions, they will be investigated for potential money laundering. As I write, 49% of all the Bitcoin 'power' is in the hands of five Chinese mining pools, so this is not difficult to imagine.

To recap: Bitcoin is not cash, because cash is fungible. If we want something to be cash, we need to make it fungible. But do we want cash? That is too complicated to go into here, but

if you want to look at some of the issues, I would strongly recommend listening to Adam Back's lecture 'Fungibility, privacy
and identity', presented at Bitcoin Israel in 2014.[*]

What happens when they get anonymous on our asses?

This is why ransomware rogues convert their Bitcoins into
something more suited to the less-regulated corners of the
economy. Whoever[†] was behind the famous WannaCry attack,
which hit more than 300,000 computers in over 150 countries,
took their rewards and converted them into Monero, a pri-
vacy-focused cryptocurrency that has seen some growth in
popularity over the last year or so. This makes me wonder
why criminals would continue to use a payment mechanism
that leaves behind a perpetual, public record of every transaction: more-private alternatives already exist in the wild.
One such example is Zcash, a cryptocurrency with the added
special sauce of genuine anonymity; this is as opposed to
pseudonymity, which, as noted, hampers the exploitation of
Bitcoin for nefarious purposes. Transactions remain confidential unless counterparties reveal their addresses by 'selective
weakening' of the cryptographic protection. I am sceptical
about whether confidential transactions will get much traction in the mass market, but that does not mean advocates of
Zcash do not have a point when they say (Peck 2016):

> If you start with a perfect electronic cash system building block,
> then you can build an electronic cash system with selective
> weakening in a way that makes sense for society.

---

* URL: https://bit.ly/38ykJ5m.
† Many people think it was the North Korean state.

You can understand why, of course. An e-cash system that is going to offer some form of privacy must be built using a truly anonymous infrastructure. There is no alternative. However, a truly anonymous infrastructure provides ample opportunities for mischief, and some of this mischief might be of significant harm to society as a whole. What will happen?

In Zcash, there are two types of addresses: 'transparent' and 'shielded'. The former, and the amounts sent to and from them, show up on the blockchain as they would in Bitcoin. If a user opts to use a shielded address, however, this will be obscured on the public ledger. If both the sender and the receiver of funds have opted to use shielded addresses, the amount sent will be encrypted as well.

Light and dark

The idea that counterparties can choose whether a transaction is visible or not is interesting and under-explored. We can use the meta-technology to construct a cash replacement system in which anonymous transactions cost more than non-anonymous transactions. One way to do this is via the Crime Pays System, or CPS, conceived by the artist Austin Houldsworth.*

It was Houldsworth's idea to have me present CPS at the British Computer Society (BCS) in 2012. In the guise of 'Mr Don Rogers', an alter ego created for the performance, I set out the new payment system to an unsuspecting audience, who, I have to say, were excellent sports about the whole

---

* Austin is, of course, most well known for designing the cover of my book *Before Babylon, Beyond Bitcoin*, but he also ran the Future of Money Design Award. Oh, and he was awarded a PhD by the Royal College of Art.

thing! It turned out to be an entertaining and enlightening experience.*

Figure 8. Crime pays.

In CPS, digital payments would be either 'light' or 'dark'. The default transaction type would be light and free to end users. All transaction histories would be uploaded to a public space (we were, of course, thinking about a blockchain here), which would allow anybody, anywhere to view the transaction details. The alternative transaction type would be dark. Under this option, advanced cryptographic techniques would make the payment completely invisible, and a small levy in the region of 10–20% would be paid per transaction.

The system would therefore offer privacy for your finances at a reasonable price. The revenue generated from the use of this system would be taken by the government to compensate for the loss of taxes in a dark economy.

---

* You can see a video of this event and read more about the idea on my blog, 15Mb: https://bit.ly/3aFtcoG.

Paradoxical pennies

Thinking this through, it seems to me that there is something of a paradox in our mental transaction models. We want our transactions to be anonymous because we are good people, but we want other people's transactions to be tracked, traced and monitored because they might be criminals. Obviously, we do not want child pornographers or terrorists to have access to anonymous e-cash, but we do want freedom fighters and oppressed minorities to. Hmm …

So, how can this paradox be resolved? One option might be to assume the anonymous cash will be used primarily by criminals, so possession of it may be taken as *prima facie* evidence of criminality, but not to ban it, because free speech trumps crime, according to our cultural values. Thus, law enforcement resources can be targeted. Remember, in an anonymous world, no one knows if you are a fraudster or if you are from the FBI. Hence, you could argue that anonymity might actually help law enforcement to carry out old-fashioned police work (and since no one knows if you are a bot either, I assume the police will implement large-scale big data analysis, pattern recognition, machine learning and all sort of other things to help them). It is not at all clear to me how the aforementioned child pornographers and terrorists will get any further beyond the reach of the law because their cash is anonymous when their mobile phone location is recorded every 50 milliseconds and their face is scanned at every street corner, but I am open to persuasion.

In the mass market, I can therefore envisage an environment where some kind of anonymous cash is in existence but is never used in its 'raw' state, because people, companies and governments will only use the privacy-enhanced layers

THE CURRENCY COLD WAR

on top of it. Getting hold of your ransomware cryptocurrency might remain easy, because companies do not carry out proper risk analyses or design secure products, but spending it could become increasingly difficult.

Secure prediction

If Bitcoin is not going to be used for money laundering, then what is it going to be used for? Certainly not to purchase goods or services, or as a store of value (except for speculators) or as a mechanism for deferred payments, since there is no real reason to imagine that it will still be around a decade from now.

Bram Cohen (the chap who invented BitTorrent) put it succinctly when he said that Bitcoin is more expensive and inconvenient than the legacy payments infrastructure, and far more expensive than that infrastructure will be when it adopts the new technology itself. This is just what the Bitcoin folk do not want to hear. As I have said before, and will say again, I think Craig Wright (the Australian who some people think is the mysterious Satoshi Nakamoto) made the key observation on this topic when he said: 'The mining of Bitcoin is a security service that alone creates no wealth. Consequently, those using the network pay for the service.'

A shared security service that people will pay to use seems like a much better way to imagine future versions of Bitcoin than as a new form of payment or as a new kind of currency. Kenneth Rogoff, former IMF chief economist, echoes this perspective (Rogoff 2016). This shared security service may be used for a great many things, most of them as yet undiscovered, and I do not doubt that people will try and possibly manage to build a viable payment service on top of it: perhaps even a full-fledged digital currency. However, I am unconvinced that Bitcoin itself will be the mass-market payment service to take on Visa and MasterCard, or the currency to replace the dollar.

No consensus

One more point about the legacy of Bitcoin. Crucial to cryptocurrencies is the possession of a mechanism for establishing *consensus* as to where money is, without having Citi in the middle to keep score. Bitcoin and similar blockchain-based cryptocurrencies, such as Ethereum, are often spoken about as implementing 'Nakamoto consensus'. This means they do not implement a complete protocol for achieving consensus about the state of the shared ledger and instead privilege the state represented by the chain that has the majority of the computing power. In other words, hash rate means hegemony. This means that it can take a while to establish consensus, which can remain probabilistic for some time (with Bitcoin, for example, people generally wait for an hour or so in order to see which chain has 'won').

Nevertheless, the science of consensus protocols is well known, highly developed and widely used to create alternatives (Kravchenko *et al.* 2018). In particular, cryptographers have been exploring what are known as Byzantine fault tolerant (BFT) protocols that use rounds of voting between participants to agree on the state of the ledger (or anything else). These protocols function as long as no more than a third of the participants are malicious. Thus, they work well when the number of participants is limited, so the voting overhead is not so great, although there are variations that allow for much larger groups of participants to interact, such as the Federated Byzantine Agreement (FBA) used in Stellar.

My general assumption, then, is that while Bitcoin has stimulated interested in using shared ledgers for money, any realistic implementation will use a limited number of trusted participants to maintain the state of the ledger, rather than rely on a centralized system (which is a vulnerability exposed frequently when bank payment networks go down) or the time and resource overheads of a Bitcoin-like form of digital money. This approach will provide for a shared ledger architecture that is, to quote Tim Swanson, 'congruent' with the financial system (Swanson 2015a).

Change agent

Ultimately, then, what is the meaning of Bitcoin? If it is not going to become the Prime or even a Patrician currency, what will it do? Yes, it has a non-zero value, but I am not sure that the price of Bitcoin actually means anything at all. As the author David Gerard is fond of saying: number go up, number go down.

Cryptocurrencies as a whole have, in fact, been falling as I have been writing this book, while Bitcoin – the original cryptocurrency – has been bouncing up and down. The economist John Kay is unconvinced that what appears to be a speculative bubble will lead to anything (Kay 2018). He writes that 'the underlying narrative of cryptocurrencies is, by the standards of historic bubbles, unusually weak; more akin to tulips than to ultimately transformational innovations such as railways or electricity'. He goes on to observe that the 'power of the current narrative is that it brings together so many features which make for an attractive and infectious story', which I think is in keeping with some observers' view of Bitcoin as a protest movement rather than a financial revolution.

I have a suspicion that Kay might be wrong, though. I think Bitcoin will have an impact and that it will lead to the creation of new markets. His mention of the railways reminded me that the cryptocurrency mania of today has mimetic echoes of the railway mania that arose after the Industrial Revolution and peaked in the mid-nineteenth century. I wrote about this back in December 2011 for *Financial World* and made the point that Victorian Britain's railway boom was truly colossal. The first railway service in the world started running between Liverpool and Manchester in 1830, and less than two decades later (by 1849), the London and North Western Railway had become the Apple of its day: one of the biggest companies on the planet.

This boom led to a massive crash in 1866. The crash was caused by the banking sector (surprise!), but in this case it was because they had been lending money to railway companies who could not pay it back, rather than to American homeowners who could not pay it back. Still, then as in our very own crash in 2007, the government had to respond. It did so by suspending the Bank Act of 1844, allowing banks to pay out in paper money rather than gold, which kept them going; however, they were not 'too big to fail', and the famous bank Overend Gurney went under. When it suspended payments after a run on 10 May 1866 (which was, as frequently noted, the last run on a British bank until the Northern Rock debacle), Overend Gurney not only ruined its own shareholders, but also caused the collapse of about 200 other companies (including other banks).*

The railway companies were huge, and a great many ordinary people had invested in them. When their directors went

---

* The directors of Overend Gurney were, incidentally, charged with fraud, but they were let off because the judge said they were merely idiots, not criminals.

to see the prime minister in 1867 to request the companies be nationalized to stop them from collapsing (because they could not pay back their loans or attract new capital),* they were not met by Gordon Brown surrounded by advisers (who happened to be bankers), tea and sympathy, followed by the suspension of competition law. Instead, they were met by Benjamin Disraeli, who told them to get stuffed. He did not see why the public should bail out badly run businesses, no matter how big they might be.

Needless to say, the economy did not collapse. As you may have noticed, we still have trains and tracks. A new railway industry was born from the ruins of the old, just as new digital currencies in both the public and private domains will rise from the ashes of Bitcoin. The transport services kept running because the new industrial economy needed them, and that economy kept on growing. The new post-industrial economy needs a new transport network, for bits rather than iron and coal, and Bitcoin's heirs and descendants might well provide it. The impact of the 1866 crash was not restricted to rail transport and the industries that used it, just as the impact of the Bitcoin crash will spread far beyond online drug dealing and mad speculation.

The introduction of basic corporate accounting standards following the collapse of the railway companies was of significant benefit to Britain and aided the development of Victorian capitalism (Odlyzko 2011). The crash not only led to a stronger railway industry, but also helped other industries, because it meant that new standards for accounting and reporting were put into place.

---

* With dreadful consequences for the whole of the British economy and in particular the widows and orphans who had invested in them.

This is hardly a novel observation. History has repeatedly gone through this cyclic coevolution of technology, business and regulation to end up with something pervasive and fundamental to the way society operates, which is why I think it is useful to make this comparison. Benoît Cœuré, chair of the Committee on Payments and Market Infrastructures (BIS), and Jacqueline Loh, chair of the Markets Committee (BIS), made this point, saying that 'while Bitcoin and its cousins are something of a mirage, they might be an early sign of change, just as PalmPilots paved the way for today's smartphones'* (Cœuré and Loh 2018).

This, I think, is the narrative that I find most plausible. But what are Bitcoin and its ilk paving the way for? I think it is new kinds of markets that trade in digital assets with no separate settlement: cryptocurrencies with an institutional link to real-world assets. These are markets made up using money-like digital bearer instruments or, as we saw in chapter 2, 'tokens'. I do not think these underlying (possibly anonymous) cryptocurrencies will be the money of the future, but instead the (not at all anonymous) 'tokens' that they support. Assuming the fallout from the Bitcoin bubble is better regulation of the platforms, then these new markets based on tokens will aid the evolution of post-modern capitalism as much as the invention of auditing helped Victorian entrepreneurs more than a century ago.

In money terms, this means that we will not be buying and selling using cryptocurrencies, but we may be using cryptocurrencies as a means to secure cryptoassets. One of the

---

* I think this comparison is even more interesting than was intended, because PayPal was originally developed as a means of using the then-new technology of infrared 'beaming' to transfer funds.

categories of cryptoassets we secure will be money that can become a digital currency.

Why digital currency?

Now let us explore why there is a demand for some form of digital currency, whether public or private, whether a fiat currency or some form of artificial currency. I rather liked the Positive Money approach to this. In a report on digital currency, Dyson and Hodgson (2016) set out what they identified as the six key benefits of the transition to digital currency. These can be labelled as innovation, inclusion and interest along with stability, seigniorage and substitutes. I will use this convenient breakdown for a discussion of these benefits, although, to be clear, I am not assuming that digital currency will be provided by a central bank.

Table 6. Benefits of a digital currency.

INNOVATION	New and better payment systems	STABILITY	Reduced risk in transactions
INCLUSION	Products and services for everyone	SEIGNIORAGE	Profits for the nation, not for the banks
INTEREST	Interest rates as an economic management tool	SUBSTITUTES	New financial instruments for the new economy

Let us take a look at each of these benefit categories in a little more detail, adding perspectives from the ECB, to try to understand whether the benefits are real and how important they might be (Bindseil 2020).

Innovation

A digital currency could promote innovation in payment systems, to the great benefit of citizens, in the face of vanishing cash and an 'overly concentrated' (an ECB phrase, not mine) retail payments sector. When looking at the options for cash replacement and reflecting on experiences with population-scale schemes such as M-Pesa in Kenya, I come to the following conclusions. It seems to me that providing a good API on top of the system and allowing innovators to build new products and services on top of that is transformational and, to my mind, much more likely to lead to real innovation, making the payment system serve the wider economy more efficiently and more effectively.

Inclusion

A digital currency could improve financial inclusion. I do not want to get into the complexities of the relationship between financial inclusion and social inclusion, and I can be extremely boring when I get talking about the relationship between digital money and digital identity, but it is clear that the framework for digital currency must interact constructively with other regulatory frameworks such as Know Your Customer (KYC) and Anti-Money Laundering (AML). I see financial inclusion through ready access to low-value digital currency accounts as one of the main reasons for wanting to move in that direction.

Remember, it is the people who are trapped on the margins in a cash economy who are the people that suffer most from its existence.

Interest

A digital currency could (as numerous central bank reports have noted, including the Bank of England's comprehensive CBDC consultation from March 2020) 'enrich the options' in a central bank's monetary policy toolkit. It would widen the reach of available monetary policy instruments by overcoming the zero-lower bound (ZLB) on interest rates, and enable the creation of new ones, such as 'helicopter money'. It should be noted that some of these gains might not be obtained without discontinuing higher denomination banknotes, which – 'although helping with AML/CTF* requirements' – would come with its own challenges. Note also that the BIS says it is 'not clear' that the current pass-through is anything but adequate: a sentiment I am not sure all economists share.

Of course, an issuer might decide to pay positive interest on digital currency balances, and there are observers who feel that in cases where the issuer is the central bank, this might simplify monetary policy.

The idea of using some form of digital currency to helicopter-drop money directly to citizens is not new (Hockett 2019a). It was, however, brought back into sharp focus because of the Covid-19 pandemic. The first draft of the Democratic Party's stimulus proposal for the United States (the 1,100-page-long Take Responsibility for Workers and Families Act) included a provision for the use of digital currency to make direct stimulus payments via a 'digital dollar wallet' that 'represents holdings in an electronic device or service that is used to store digital dollars that may be tied

---

* Counter-terrorist financing.

to a **digital [identity]** or physical identity' (my emphasis). These digital dollars did not make it through to the final 1,400-page version of the proposal.

They did, however, reappear in a bill put forward by Senator Sherrod Brown (D-OH), ranking member of the Senate Committee on Banking, Housing, and Urban Affairs. The bill called for a scheme in which citizens could set up a digital dollar wallet, called a FedAccount. This wallet would be opened remotely, in accordance with Financial Action Task Force (FATF) guidance on remote digital onboarding issued in March 2020 (FATF 2020), through local banks and post offices. The assumption, I imagine, was that with instant digital onboarding the vast majority of the population ought to be able to enrol in a couple of minutes, download a Fed app and get to work. FedAccounts could then be used to ensure that everyone who was entitled to Covid-19-related relief would receive it quickly and inexpensively. I completely sympathize with the spirit of the senator's proposal, but would people really have accounts with or devices from the Fed, or any other central bank? I think not, as I will explain in chapter 6.

It would be an interesting turn of events, to say the least, if the Covid-19 crisis turned out to be a trigger for the transition to digital currency in developed nations, particularly in the United States, where the spectacle of the government mailing paper cheques to desperate citizens seems oddly anachronistic. As the Brookings Institution puts it (Klein 2020):

> How is it that our government is unable to directly pay such a large share of the American people during a time of crisis without waiting over a month to send a paper check?

Seigniorage

A digital currency could allow a central bank to recapture a portion of seigniorage. As I mentioned earlier, seigniorage is the income earned on currency issue. A £50 note does not cost £50 to make, so if £50 notes are replaced by digital currency, and the banks stop buying them because people stop using them, the Bank of England's profits would tumble. We will return to this point when we discuss currency boards later on.

Calculations in the United Kingdom show that the Bank of England might roughly double its seigniorage revenue if most people switched most of their spending from bank accounts to digital cash. This issue is more acute in the United States, being, as it is, at the top of the currency pyramid and collecting, as the *Wall Street Journal* puts it, 'enormous' seigniorage revenues from the rest of the world (Raskin and Yermack 2016). To give you more of a feeling for the dynamics, note that, over the last few decades, the value of dollars in circulation has grown at around 7% per annum (one to two percentage points more than GDP), with overall currency movements being dominated by $100 bills. The demand for $50 and $100 bills is still strong but does seem to be slowing. The amount of US currency in circulation is around $1.5 trillion (of which $1.2 trillion is in the form of those $100 bills), and official estimates are that more than half of this is outside the United States (Judson 2017).

For the euro area as a whole, estimates of the private seigniorage earned by commercial banks are in the region of €100 billion (yes, billion).

Substitute

A digital currency could be used to create alternative financial instruments as substitutes for conventional bank loans. Separating the creation of money from bank loans might mean a reduction in lending, which would have implications for the economy. There will also be consequences for banks regarding the supply of credit as well as the potential for new kinds of financial products to replace those loans.

This takes us into the world of decentralized finance discussed earlier, which I am not framing as either good or bad here, because it is neither. In a European Parliament report, Fiedler *et al.* (2018) noted the implications of market participants shifting liquidity away from bank deposits to digital currencies, saying that the 'current fractional reserve banking system would be challenged at its core'. Their report points out that commercial banks would need to come up with funding sources other than deposits, but 'as the fractional reserve character of the current banking system can be a major source of instability', this might not be a bad thing: quite the contrary, in fact. Without getting sidetracked discussing what the DeFi system might look like, it is fair to observe that it is hardly a fringe view that substituting new and better instruments for bank credit might actually pave the way for a more stable financial system.

Stability

A digital currency could increase financial stability by providing a risk-free alternative to bank accounts. This would boost stability by easing the concentration of liquidity risk and credit risk via, as an ECB working paper puts it, reducing moral hazard by downscaling banks (Bindseil 2020). This means that commercial banks would become credit brokers rather than credit creators, losing the private seigniorage attendant on credit creation. As a non-economist, I can see the attraction of reducing the systemic importance of 'too big to fail' institutions in order to abate the externalities stemming from potential instability in the banking system.

This is not all about the stability of banks, though. Non-bank financial institutions in particular would benefit from being able to hold funds in central bank money as opposed to in the form of an uninsured bank account.

Incidentally, Dyson and Hodgson (2016) remark that the existence of digital fiat (as we will see in chapter 6) might well exacerbate bank runs, as people, for whatever reason, retreat from other forms of liquidity to risk-free central bank money. The existence of risk-free digital currency in the United Kingdom could plausibly lead to an inflow of funds from foreign banks in sterling digital cash, and that, in turn, could push up exchange rates.

Digital currency from the central bank is only one kind of stable digital currency, however. There are others that should be explored, so let us take a look at all of them in some more detail.

Exploring stability

There is an underlying assumption that any practical digital currency based on some form of cryptocurrency would need to demonstrate that it is reasonably stable in order to obtain hegemony. Hence the term 'stablecoin', which is being bandied about by Libra and others. But what does it actually *mean*? The Bank of England's excellent *Bank Underground* blog explains that there are generally two designs of stablecoin: those that are backed by assets and those that are unbacked or 'algorithmic' (Dyson 2019). This is right, of course, but I would like to present a slightly more granular classification of stablecoin currencies. Barry Eichengreen of UC Berkeley identifies four kinds, as shown in table 7 (Eichengreen 2019). I will use his helpful breakdown here.

Table 7. Categories of stablecoins.

CATEGORIZATION	BACKING	EXAMPLE
Fully collateralized	Assets (including 'tier 1' capital and fiat currencies)	Libra, e-Krona
Cryptocollateralized	Cryptocurrencies	Dai
Uncollateralized	Algorithms	Basis
Partially collateralized	Assets and algorithms	Saga

There are already instances of each of these approaches being tried in different contexts and at different times, so while it is still early days, we can look at some of these examples for illumination.

A fully collateralized stablecoin: e-Krona

Collateralization includes 'self-collateralization', where a central bank creates a digital currency as a claim on itself. One such experiment already in progress is the Swedish central bank's e-Krona pilot project, which I discussed earlier.

A cryptocollateralized stablecoin: Dai

The first attempt to scale a stablecoin came from Maker. At the time of writing, there are about half a billion dollars worth of cryptocurrency tied up as collateral for this stablecoin – the Dai – whose value is pegged to the US dollar. The peg operates through feedback loops using collateralized debt positions (CDPs). With a CDP, a user deposits a cryptoasset into a smart contract as collateral for a loan. Once the CDP holds the assets deposited by a user, that user can then borrow up to two-thirds of the equivalent US dollar value in Dai. Users can trade it, pay with it, or do whatever they want to do with Dai.

The deposited assets inside a CDP can only be retrieved once the user has paid back the same amount of Dai they initially borrowed. However, generating the initial CDP to borrow Dai also accrues interest, so the user must pay back the Dai they borrowed plus the generated interest to retrieve their assets. Active CDPs must always hold a higher collateral value than the value of debt the user has. CDPs that hold less value in collateral than they do in debt risk being liquidated (with a 13% penalty) and sold off.

The algorithms used to try to hold the value of one Dai at $1 are too complicated to go into here, but suffice it to say that they are based on adjusting the supply of Dai according to the demand for it (DiPrisco 2017).

An uncollateralized stablecoin: Basis

Basis, originally known as Basiscoin, was an attempt to build a stablecoin wholly supported by algorithms as opposed to assets. It was a well-funded start-up (with $100 million plus from Google Ventures, Andreessen Horowitz, Bain Capital and others) that ended up shutting down and returning all of its remaining funds to investors back in 2018.

This enterprise had the interesting idea of creating an 'algorithmic central bank' that would deliver a stable currency (Castillo 2018a). By automatically buying back Basis tokens when their price dropped and minting new tokens when their price increased, the algorithm's creators hoped to provide a new global currency. In the end, however, they found the regulatory problems (specifically, regulatory uncertainty) to be an insurmountable barrier.

A partially collateralized stablecoin: Saga

An example of a stablecoin that illustrates a few of these design choices rather well is Saga (or SGA). This was launched at the end of 2019 by a team that includes a couple of former central bankers from the Bank of Israel (Hinge 2019b).

SGA is partly backed by a reserve (which shadows the SDR basket). At the launch of the currency, the reserve was 100%, but the idea is that, as the value of the currency in circulation rises, the reserve will become fractional (the concept behind this is that, as the trust in the currency rises, the need for a reserve falls away). The company will manage the amount of currency in circulation 'algorithmically' to maintain its value.*

It has an interesting governance structure, designed to ensure holders of the currency have a say in operations.

---

* This claim was met with scepticism by some observers, including the head of digitalization at the Bank of Finland, who commented: 'it is clear, of course, that Saga is issued by them, and that it is governed by them, not code or algorithms'. He also claimed that Saga is using this structure 'as a means of avoiding regulation'.

THE CURRENCY COLD WAR

Holders of SGA are permitted to appoint members to an assembly that can dismiss SGA's executive council, and there is a monetary committee that oversees the smart contract which governs SGA's monetary policy.

SGA requires users to go through a proper KYC check, thereby allaying the money-laundering concerns that are common with digital currencies.

Maintaining stability

Using this breakdown, and assuming that partially collateralized currencies will struggle to gain confidence and that collateralization by crypto is an unproven (and potentially dangerous) model, I think we should focus on three main mechanisms to deliver a stable currency.

Algorithms, in which algorithms manage supply and demand to obtain stability of the digital currency. This is what a real stable cryptocurrency would be. Since a cryptocurrency is backed by nothing other than mathematics, it is mathematics that manages the money supply to hold the value steady against some external benchmark.*

Assets, in which an asset or basket of assets is used to back the digital currency. I do not know why people refer to these as stablecoins, since they are stable only against the specific assets that back them: an asset that is backed by, say, crude oil is stable against crude oil but nothing else.

Currencies (aka currency boards, which we will discuss later), which are similar to asset-backed currencies, but in this case the assets backing the digital currency are fiat currencies

---

* This is also what was meant by 'stablecoin' in the original crypto use of the term.

only. There are mundane versions of these already: in Bulgaria, for example, the local currency (the Lev) is backed by a 100% reserve of euros.

As regards the last category, this is effectively what is currently defined as e-money under the existing EU directives, and therefore it is already regulated. The cryptocoins backed by fiat currency, such as JPM Coin, simply provide a convenient way to transfer value around the internet without having to go through banking networks. Now, this may well be an advantage in terms of cost and convenience in some use cases, but it is a long way from the stablecoin as it was originally envisioned.

In November 2019, the head of the Financial Crimes Enforcement Network (FinCEN) made it clear that, as US regulators are technology neutral, transactions using any of these kinds of stablecoin are covered by the Bank Secrecy Act (BSA), and that, for AML/CTF purposes, the administrators of any such services have to register as Money Services Businesses (MSBs) with FinCEN (2019). In the United Kingdom, the recent adoption of the Money Laundering and Terrorist Financing (Amendment) Regulations 2019 goes beyond the requirements of the EU's Fifth Anti-Money Laundering Directive (AMLDV), adopted by member states in January 2020, to require all 'cryptoasset' businesses to comply with national AML/CTF regulations. The new markets are shaping up.

With this level of regulatory scrutiny (and overhead), will any of these types of currencies catch on?

Predictions are, of course, difficult, but my general feeling is that it is the asset-backed currencies that are most interesting and most likely to succeed in causing an actual revolution in finance and banking. Algorithmic stablecoins and fiat 'stablecoins' exist to serve a demand for value transfer, but this is increasingly being served – and well – by conventional means. I have noticed, for example, that TransferWise can now send money from the United Kingdom to Hong Kong in 11 seconds, a feat that is only made possible by its direct connection to the payment networks of both countries. Why would I use a fiat token when I can send fiat money faster and for less?

Of course, you might argue that a digital currency board would allow people who are excluded from the global financial system to hold and transfer value, but I remain unconvinced. There are plenty of ways to hold and transfer electronic value (e.g. M-Pesa) without using bank accounts. Generally speaking, people around the world are excluded because of regulation (e.g. KYC), so if we want to do something about inclusion, we should probably start there. If you are going to require KYC for the electronic wallet needed to hold your digital currency, then customers might just as well open a bank account, right?

I suppose there are some people who think that the anonymity and pseudonymity of cryptocurrencies might make them an attractive alternative for certain sectors, but this is probably a window that will be closed in time by a combination of law and good business practice. If cryptocurrencies were used for crime on a large scale, then efforts would be made to police them. Bitcoin in particular is not a good choice for criminals, since it leaves a public, immutable record of their actions; but one can imagine a future in which the mere possession of an anonymous cryptocurrency becomes a *prima facie* case for money laundering.

Looking at the 'stable' part of stablecoins, then, I am putting my money on the second mechanism. There is a real marketplace logic to the trading of asset-backed currencies in the form of tokens, and I expect to see an explosion of different kinds. Assuming that one important category of asset is central bank money, this analysis suggests that the competition that needs to be considered will be between private asset-based currencies and public fiat-backed (or synthetic) currencies.

Chapter 5

Rethinking money

The instruments of trade and finance are inventions – products of the human imagination.

— John Lanchester, writing for *The New Yorker* (July 2019)

If the current IMFS is coming to an end, and new technology means we can start thinking about alternatives, what will the narrative of our new money be? By this, I mean what story will we tell to understand our new money and the way it works? At Sibos 2019 London, a global banking conference, my good friend Brett King (author of the seminal *Bank 2.0*) and I challenged the audience to contemplate what is on the horizon by looking at how writers have thought about the future of payments, banking and money. I find this is a useful backdrop to help us formulate strategies in this space.

The following is an example I often quote. It is taken from a narrative I found so interesting that I discussed it at length in my previous book. It is a work of utopian future fiction that happens to have something interesting to say about money, which is why it caught my eye. This is somewhat unusual for a utopian vision, since, as Nigel Dodd observed in his 2014 book *The Social Life of Money*, utopias – from Plato's *Republic* to *Star Trek* – do not usually seem to include money at all, never mind M-Pesa or Bitcoin.

Anyhow, the story that interested me has a 'guy falls asleep under hypnosis, wakes up a century later to find a model society, and then finds out it is all a dream' narrative arc that is hard to read with modern eyes, because the perfect society the author imagines is a communist superstate that looks like Disneyland run by Stalin. Everyone works for the government, and since government planners can optimize production, the 'inefficiency' of the free market is gone.

During his adventures in this new world, our time-travelling protagonist, who doubles as the narrator, is told by his host in the modern era (the good Doctor Edward Leete) that cash no longer exists. Instead, Dr Leete informs him, the populace uses 'credit cards' for retail transactions.*

While the author does not talk about the telephone, laser beams or the knowledge economy, he does make insightful predictions about the evolution of money. When talking about an American going to visit Berlin, Dr Leete notes how convenient it is for international travellers to use these 'credit cards' instead of foreign currency: 'An American credit card,' says Dr Leete, 'is just as good as American gold used to be.'

This is an excellent description of our world after the end of the gold standard. A clever prediction. However, I think the most fascinating insight into the future of money comes later in the book, when the time traveller asks his twenty-first-century host: 'Are credit cards issued to the women just as to the men?' Dr Leete replies 'certainly'.

That answer might alert you to the age of the text, which actually contains the earliest mention of a credit card that I have found anywhere as part of a fictional narrative. The

---

* He then goes on to describe what are in fact offline pre-authorized debit cards imagined in the technology of the day, but that is by the by.

book is by the American author Edward Bellamy and is called *Looking Backward, 2000–1887*. It was written in 1886, a century before the credit card became an iconic representation of modern money, and it was one of the best-selling books of its day.

I cannot help but reflect that the discourse on money in that book is a wonderful example of how science fiction is not really about the future at all but about the present. The retort 'certainly' is clearly intended to surprise the Victorian reader as much as, if not more than, the author's vision of glass tunnels that surround pavements when it rains. It took a writer, not an economist or a technologist, to ask a simple question about money and get an innovative answer. Hold that thought.

Predictions are hard, especially about the future of money

Now, let us have a go at predicting what money will look like half a century from now. Where do we start? Well, a good rule of thumb for futurologists is that if you want to look 50 years forward, you need to look at least 100 years back because of the increasing pace of change. A century ago, we had the telephone and global markets connected by instant, global communications. We had the Bank of England and the Federal Reserve. We had wire transfers. We had the world's first commercial aviation service, created, as it happens, to accelerate the clearing of cheques between Chicago and New York.

A century ago, we were also coming to the end of the era of the classical gold standard. The demise of that global financial system was brought about by the pressures of global conflict and depression, which ultimately led Britain to abandon it permanently in 1931 after a temporary suspension that began in the middle of World War I and lasted until 1925. After World War II, we had the Bretton Woods system, named after the resort where a gathering of 730 delegates* from the 44 Allied nations worked out the IMFS for a new peaceful world (Conway 2014). Bretton Woods lasted until 1973, when the European countries that were still tied to the US dollar announced they would sever the link. The system was over, replaced by what economists have since labelled the Bretton Woods II era.

This era has been one in which the US dollar dominated international trade, was kept overvalued by emerging-market purchases and boosted the competitiveness of emerging-market exporters. The United States itself has run up large and persistent current account deficits. In essence, the United States's excessive consumption has been funded by lending from the emerging world, which invested in American assets. The overall flow of greenbacks was from American consumers out to reserve-accumulating exporters (mainly in China), and from them via lending (e.g. from US Treasuries) back to America to fund more imports and so on.

Many people think we are now coming to the end of that era. As *The Economist* observed recently (*Economist* 2019b), international trade is complicated because 'most countries have their own currencies, which move in idiosyncratic ways and can be held down to boost competitiveness'. In other words, it is not at all clear what is coming next!

If we set aside both the misplaced view that the status quo will prevail and the Bitcoin maximalists' fantasies of a completely decentralized society, where do we look to find

---

* The United Kingdom's delegate was John Maynard Keynes.

believable alternatives? We all hear the speeches of the regulators, read the annual reports of the bankers, watch the demos of the technologists and applaud the slide decks of the entrepreneurs. But have any of these created a vision in your mind? Perhaps it is time to return to my opening observations: to develop a narrative that will be just as surprising to a contemporary audience as Bellamy's was to a Victorian one.

Science (fiction), bitch

So, what do we expect to see a couple of generations from now? A world like that of Star Wars, with a 'galactic credit' that is universally accepted? That does not seem right to me. If we cannot quite get a single currency to work between Germany and Greece, how would it work between Earth and LV-426? Would the use of a synthetic hegemonic currency (SHC) as envisaged by Mark Carney function in these circumstances as a trade currency for the universe?

A world like that of Star Trek, then, with no money at all save the gold-pressed latinum of the Ferengi, valuable because it is the only substance that the replicators cannot produce? Or a financial system based on Charles Stross's Neptune's Brood, where there is fast money and there is slow money that relies on cryptography, so it only travels at one-third the speed of light?

How will people conduct transactions? Will we take a leaf from Robert Heinlein's Beyond the Horizon, where the government has an 'integrated accumulator' (what we would now call a permissioned shared ledger) to record all transactions, and the finance minister has a dashboard that lets him see how the economy is doing? The integrated accumulator sounds very much like the 'compubank' in Margaret Atwood's *The Handmaid's Tale*, which details what could happen if such machinery fell into the hands of fanatics: in the case of Atwood's book, a theocratic US administration that bans and blocks women's payment cards. Will cash, indeed, be banned, or will it simply be regarded as in William Gibson's *Count Zero*? Here, the protagonist finds himself in a near future where he 'had his cash money, but you couldn't pay for food with that. It wasn't actually illegal to have the stuff, it was just that nobody ever did anything legitimate with it.'*

What if money as we know it vanishes as a medium of exchange? Might we find ourselves in the world of Bruce Sterling's *Distraction*, where distributed servers manage reputation as currency? This theme is also present in Cory Doctorow's *Down and Out in the Magic Kingdom*. I am naturally attracted to these images of a future in which identity, trust and reputation reconnect us with our neolithic heritage (a central theme of my 2014 book *Identity Is the New Money*) and we have dispensed with many kinds of intermediaries. Will this free us or will it fulfil the prophecy of the Book of Revelation 13:16–17 that 'no man might buy or sell save that he has the mark, or the name of the beast, or the number of his name'? Should we begin our scenario planning for these transactional environments now (hint: the answer is yes) or should we leave the technologists to choose a future for us?

Moving to synthetic currency

This, of course, moves us on to a bigger picture. Technologists are not, or at least should not be, the only people who are

---

* Which, frankly, sounds like Sweden rather than some future dystopia.

rethinking money in light of new technology. The narrative needs to be created by a much wider spectrum of people. Digital currency is a political issue as much as a technological one. This was made plain when Mark Carney, governor of the Bank of England, gave a speech at Jackson Hole, Wyoming, in which he said that a form of global digital currency could be 'the answer to the destabilising dominance of the US dollar in today's global monetary system' (Giles 2019). The problem he is alluding to is that the US dollar's global electronic hegemony 'made sense after World War II, when the [United States] accounted for 28% of global exports'. Now, however, that figure is 8.8%, according to the IMF. 'Yet the dollar still dominates international trade' (Michaels and Vigna 2019). This means demand for the US dollar and dollar-denominated instruments remains artificially high, so the dollar is still the world's reserve currency, even though the United States's share of global GDP has approximately halved in the last 60 years (figure 9).

Figure 9. United States's share of global GDP.

The US dollar is involved in around 9 in 10 FX trades (compared with around 1 in 25 for China's renminbi), and BIS figures show that non-US banks hold some $12 trillion in dollar assets (of which China accounts for a trillion) that must be funded with dollar liabilities. The US dollar's dominance as a transaction currency has serious implications (Sandbu 2020). One of them is that global trade, in a globalized world of global supply chains, is held back by a strong US dollar. These long supply chains, constructed to deliver efficiency within industries, have significant financing requirements for importers and exporters. It appears this often takes the form of dollar lending to companies outside the United States who transact in dollars.

The availability of such credit varies with the exchange rate, so when dollars are less expensive, banks lend more of them. Thus, a stronger dollar makes it more expensive to finance cross-border value chains, which holds back trade growth and therefore prosperity (Bruno and Shin 2019).

Another problem is that a strong US dollar worsens the terms of trade for (non-US) trading countries. Yet *another* problem is that it hurts the finances of emerging economies (who borrow in dollars). All round, it seems, the demand for US dollars as a transactional currency has considerable negative ramifications, hence Carney's remarks.

In his speech, Carney went on to talk about the idea of SHC mentioned earlier. This is a form of alternative currency unit (ACU), a concept that has a long heritage (Ascheim and Park 1976). There are, broadly speaking, two kinds of ACUs: those created by official institutions, primarily for official international transactions; and those introduced at the initiative of private companies for commercial transactions. The pre-eminent example of the former category is the IMF's special drawing right (SDR).

The SDR (which, confusingly, has the ISO 4217 code 'XDR') was created as a supplementary international reserve asset in the context of the Bretton Woods fixed exchange rate system. After the collapse of that system in 1973, the shift of major currencies towards floating exchange rate regimes lessened our reliance on the SDR as a global reserve asset. It was initially defined as equivalent to 0.888671 grams of fine gold, which, at the time, was equivalent to one US dollar. In 1973, the SDR was redefined as a basket of currencies. This basket (last reviewed in 2015) is made up of five major world currencies, as shown in table 8.

Table 8. The SDR basket.

CURRENCY	ISO 4217	WEIGHT
US dollar	USD	41.73%
Euro	EUR	30.93%
Chinese yuan	CNY	10.92%
Japanese yen	JPY	8.33%
Pound sterling	GBP	8.09%

The SDR is therefore neither a currency nor a claim on the IMF. Rather, it is a potential claim on the freely usable currencies of IMF members, as SDRs can be exchanged for these currencies. In addition, the SDR serves as the unit of account for the IMF and a number of other international organizations (e.g. the Asian Development Bank). It is also used in some international agreements: to give an example, the Convention on Limitation of Liability for Maritime Claims sets limits in XDR.

There are other examples of ACUs, both private and public. The European Currency Unit (ECU), the precursor to the euro, could have used the new digital money technology to become a 'hard e-Euro' for cross-border trade. I assume that

Carney was thinking of these kinds of 'official' ACUs when he said (Jeffery and Hinge 2019):

> We think Libra and other potential new payment solutions are shining a light on deficiencies in the system. And that is to be welcomed. They are trying to solve them. So domestic payments are still too slow and not distributed in real time. And cross-border payments are much worse. They cost a lot more and take a lot longer to execute. And that is just not necessary. It is a product of the old architecture. So coming up with new architecture and trying to solve it is a good thing.

He went on to say that his central bank serves 'the people of the United Kingdom through the financial system' and that 'we do not serve the banks and insurance companies *per se*, they are financial intermediaries that also serve the financial system'.

An obvious example of the kind of ACU-as-SHC that Carney envisages, created by an official institution for international transactions, would be an electronic version of the SDR. In fact, the World Bank's former boss of SDRs has already put forward such a proposal, asking for the IMF to develop a procedure for issuing and using market SDRs following 'currency board' rules (we will come to what a currency board is shortly) and 'backed 100% by official SDRs or by an appropriate mix of sovereign debt of the five basket currencies' (Coats 2019).

Currency boards

As noted in the discussion about types of digital currency, a digital fiat currency that is 100% backed by a basket of other currencies is known as a 'currency board'. These are not new;

in fact, the currency board system was once quite widespread. It was used in approximately 65 countries, having seen something of a revival in the last century (Hanke and Schuler 1998).

The currency board itself is an institution that issues money (which used to be notes and coins, of course, but we are only interested in digital money) which can be converted into external 'reserve' assets such as other fiat currencies or some commodity on demand at a fixed exchange rate. The currency board's reserves are equal to 100%, or perhaps even slightly more, of the digital money that is put into circulation. The institution generates profits (seigniorage) from the difference between the interest earned on the securities that it holds and the expense of creating and maintaining the digital currency. Historically, currency boards tended to be run by governments, so all profits beyond what were needed to cover the expenses of issuing the currency were remitted back to the government.

The currency board has no discretion and no independent monetary policy. It is subservient to the monetary policy of whoever manages the supply of whatever the reserve asset or assets happen to be. This is, generally speaking, a good thing, since if a Plebeian currency were being managed properly there would not be a currency board in place.

The use of a stable currency brings significant economic benefits. An often-used example is that of Zimbabwe, where the government introduced a 'multi-currency' system in February 2009, with the US dollar becoming the official currency. This led to all sectors in the economy experiencing improvements, with real GDP swinging from −15% to +6% within a year. A stable and predictable exchange rate policy and appropriate management of monetary policy lead to macroeconomic stability and economic growth (Townsend 2018c). The lesson we learnt in the case of Zimbabwe's economic crisis was that having a stable exchange rate and a stable currency benefits countries that experience hyperinflation.

When a currency board is based on a foreign currency, using its digital currency is much like using that foreign currency directly for domestic transactions, except that it captures for domestic benefit the seigniorage that would otherwise accrue to the foreign issuer. This is in contrast to the dollarization just discussed, or the permeation of economies where it is the US dollar that circulates. If there were a digital US dollar, it would perform a similar function in online transactions, so the seigniorage would continue to flow to the United States. Thus, in the case of a developing country with an unstable currency, that country would obtain the benefits of dollarization without ceding seigniorage, which can be substantial. Studies vary, but the Federal Reserve estimates that some two-thirds of US currency circulates outside of America and is unlikely to ever return. That represents quite a big interest-free loan to Uncle Sam from the rest of the world.

In practice, currency board systems have an excellent track record. They depoliticize the supply of money by not leaving it exclusively to the government or the private sector to control, and they protect the economy by requiring full reserves and external assets.

Digital currency: the Ecuadorian dollar

An interesting experiment in creating a digital currency took place in Latin America when the Central Bank of Ecuador (BCE) launched a national mobile payment scheme. Since the US dollar has been legal tender in Ecuador since 2000, when the post-gold standard 'sucre' was abandoned, the mobile payment scheme was similarly denominated.

Remember my point about transferring seigniorage? This was the driver here. The US Federal Reserve banknotes that are in circulation in Ecuador are, in essence, an interest-free loan. By replacing these through a digital currency board, the BCE hoped to reclaim the seigniorage.

For a currency board to succeed, it has to be trusted, obviously. This trust is rooted in transparency. If the assets are there, then the users of the currency – consumers and businesses – will happily exchange the digital currency. If, however, the managers of the currency board were to issue digital currency against assets that are not there, then the currency would fall by the wayside, and Ecuador would be unable to reap the many benefits of the transition away from cash (*Economist* 2014b).

In the case of Ecuador, the lack of transparency, and therefore the lack of faith from the populace, led to the system being abandoned in December 2017; this was when Ecuador's National Assembly decommissioned the system and opened the market to mobile payment alternatives from the country's private commercial banks and savings institutions (White 2018).

Zimbabwe provides a similar lesson. At the beginning of 2019, the real-time gross settlement (RTGS) dollar (which was issued against US dollars held in a bank account) was adopted as a Zimbabwean currency, alongside 'bond notes' and foreign currencies. By the middle of that year, the use of foreign currencies was outlawed for most transactions. Since the banks lacked the US dollar reserves needed to maintain the convertibility of the RTGS dollar, the value of these digital dollars started to collapse, dropping from 2.5 to the US dollar to 25 to the US dollar on the black market at the end of 2019.

Transnational physical currency: the CFA franc

Originally the 'Franc of the French Colonies in Africa', renamed the Franc of the Financial Community of Africa (CFA), this title actually covers two currencies: the West African CFA franc (XOF) and the Central African CFA franc (XAF). They were created in 1945 when France· ratified the Bretton Woods agreement.

- The West African CFA franc is issued by the Central Bank of West African States in Dakar, Senegal, and is used by the Ivory Coast, Senegal, Mali, Burkina Faso, Benin, Niger, Togo and Guinea-Bissau.

- The Central African CFA franc is issued by the Bank of Central African States in Yaoundé, Cameroon.

Although separate, these two currencies were always at parity and are to all intents and purposes interchangeable. Both were guaranteed by their respective countries' deposits of reserves at the French Treasury, on which they were paid 0.75% interest.

It should be noted that I am not qualified to comment on the political economy of the CFA franc. Supporters claim that it has provided stability and saved the countries that use it from inflation. Critics observe that it is a strong currency that makes exports from the mostly underdeveloped and agricultural countries in its zone more expensive than they would otherwise be, because the currency cannot devalue, and it therefore restricts economic growth.

The CFA franc effectively maintained a quasi-colonial trading relationship between France and its former African colonies. However, in what has been dubbed 'West Africa's Brexit' by the *Financial Times*, XOF is going to be replaced by a new currency called the 'eco', and it is assumed that XAF will go down the same path (Pilling 2020). This means that the countries using XOF will no longer have to keep half their reserves in France or have a French emissary occupying a seat on their central banks' boards. The eco will remain pegged to the euro and guaranteed by France (a peg that will surely be tested in a time of crisis), but this nevertheless represents a significant step away from the continent's colonial past.

It is interesting to note that the East African Community (EAC) Partner States – Burundi, Kenya, Rwanda, South Sudan, Tanzania and Uganda – have decided to put in place the institutions needed to create a single currency for their region within the next five years. This plan, set out in the EAC's Monetary Union Protocol, includes the establishment of an East African Monetary Institute (EAMI), with the intention of turning this into an East African Central Bank somewhere down the line.

Transnational digital currency: the hard ECU

When she was head of the IMF and a pillar of the Washington Consensus – and therefore, to a first approximation, the woman in charge of money – Christine Lagarde gave a talk at the 2017 Bank of England conference on central banking and fintech. In it, she said that virtual currencies (by which she means digital currencies, in my taxonomy) could actually become more stable than fiat currencies (Lagarde 2017). She explained that, 'for instance, they could be issued one-for-one for dollars, or a stable basket of currencies'.

This is an interesting idea, but it is not a new one. Many years ago, John Major, then UK Chancellor of the Exchequer (chief financial minister), proposed just such a sensible alternative to the euro, which at the time was labelled the 'hard ECU'.

The idea behind this hard ECU was to have a pan-European digital currency (it would never exist in physical form) that was accepted in all member states. I am not alone in thinking this was a missed opportunity. Keith Hart, author of the brilliant *The Memory Bank*, a book about money from an anthropological perspective, wrote that it was a big mistake to replace national currencies with the euro. He further pointed out (and this was back in 2012) that the hard ECU would have meant politically managed fiat currencies alongside a low-inflation alternative: a plural option that could be enjoyed by countries which did not join the euro, such as Britain and Switzerland (Hart 2012). I could not agree with him more.

The hard ECU – or, as I used to like calling it, the e-ECU – was always a better idea than the euro, but when John Major proposed it, he was ignored. Major envisaged a cross-border currency that businesses and tourists could use. The former could keep accounts in hard ECUs and trade them all over Europe, with minimal transaction costs and no FX risk, while the latter could have hard ECU payment cards they could use across the continent. Each state would continue with its own national currency – in the United Kingdom, for instance, you would still be able to use sterling notes and coins as well as sterling-denominated cards – so the cost of replacing it would have been saved.

This idea actually goes back to the days before Lagarde and Major, to the beginnings of Margaret Thatcher's government and a 1983 report by the European Parliament on the European monetary system. The proposal was, at that time, supported across political and national groups in the parliament, including by the Germans, so long as the central bank only concerned itself with the stability of the currency (as subsequently transpired). It was taken up by Thatcher's government as a practical single currency for Europe: a means of expanding the United Kingdom's financial services industry across a European single market. Yet concept never became reality, and the political drive for the euro later on saw this idea sidelined for good.

The point is, though, that it was a feasible option, and that a digital currency backed by a fiat currency reserve is both a sensible idea and a potential hegemonic currency.

Exploring taxonomy: the Dimon dollar

To illustrate some of the points I made about types of money using the technology platform discussed earlier, I will cite the example of the JPM Coin. Back in 2019, the media reported – somewhat breathlessly, as I recall – that JPMorgan Chase (JPMC) was launching a 'cryptocurrency to transform the payments business'. As CNBC reported at the time, the announcement seemed to herald new forms of business. Umar Farooq, the head of JPMC's blockchain projects, set out the vision clearly, saying the applications of this innovative use of new transaction technologies were 'frankly quite endless; anything where you have a distributed ledger which involves corporations or institutions [could] use this' (see Son 2019).

Many people took a look at the initiative and pointed out that it was simply JPMC deposits by another name. Some uncharitable persons (of whom I was not one) dismissed it as a marketing gimmick. But it was more interesting than a marketing gimmick, and I think it is helpful to explore *why* in

THE CURRENCY COLD WAR

order to give the issues of cryptocurrency and tokens some context in the IMFS.

We will start with the problem it was trying to solve. Suppose I am running apps (referred to by less well-informed industry commentators as 'smart contracts') on JPMC's Quorum blockchain. Quorum is the company's double-permissioned Ethereum fork (that is, it requires permission to access it and further permission to take part in the consensus-forming process). I am interested in Quorum and always curious to see how it is developing and helping to define what I call the enterprise shared ledger (ESL) software category. Suppose now that my Quorum app wants to make a payment, not in imaginary internet money but in US dollars, in return for some service. How can it do this? ESL apps cannot send a wire transfer or use a credit card, because they can only access data on the ledger. If the app has to pay using a credit card, and that app could be executing on a thousand nodes in the ESL network, then we end up with a thousand credit card payments all being fired off within a few seconds of each other. You can see why this would not work!

One way to solve this general class of problem is to have 'oracles' reporting on the state of bank accounts to the ledger and 'watchers' (or 'custom executors', as I have seen them called) looking for state changes in the ledger shadows of bank accounts, so they could then instruct matching changes in the actual bank accounts. However, that would mean putting the safe-to-spend limits for millions of bank accounts onto the ledger.

Another, more practical, solution would be to add tokens to Quorum and allow the apps to send these tokens to one another. This was, as far as I could tell from a distance, the purpose of JPM Coins. I have to say that this is a fairly standard way of approaching the problem, and JPMC is not the first company to exploit such a solution. Signature Bank in New York launched just such a service for corporate customers, with a minimum $250,000 balance, using a similar permissioned Ethereum fork that converted Uncle Sam's dollars into ERC-20 tokens (Castillo 2018b).*

These JPM Coins (I could not resist calling them Dimon dollars, or $Dimon, for obvious reasons) generated considerable discussion, not least at the Berlin Merchant Payments Ecosystem Conference in 2018, where I said that the right way to see $Dimon is as e-money. My reasoning, which I hope will inform the analysis later in this book, was as follows.

- Is it 'money'? No, it is not. It is certainly a cryptoasset (that is, a digital asset that has an institutional binding to a real-world asset, which, in certain circumstances, exhibits money-like behaviour). Personally, I am happy to classify such assets as forms of digital money, my logic being that they are bearer instruments that can be traded without clearing or settlement.

- Is it a 'cryptocurrency'? No, it is not. A cryptocurrency has its value determined, essentially, by mathematics, in that the algorithm which produces the currency is known and the value of the cryptocurrency depends only on the known supply and the unknown demand (and, of course, on market manipulation of various kinds). It is not set by an institution, government or otherwise.

* If you are particularly interested, I gave a presentation at the Dutch Blockchain Innovation Conference 2018 on this approach and why I thought it would grow. The video is available online at http://bit.ly/30wa4pe.

THE CURRENCY COLD WAR

- Is it a 'stablecoin'? No, it is not. A stablecoin has its value maintained at a certain level with reference to a fiat currency by managing the supply of the coins. The value of the $Dimon, however, is maintained by JPMC, irrespective of the demand for it.

- Is it a 'currency board'? No, it is not. A currency board, as noted, maintains the value of one currency using a reserve in another currency. For example, you might have a Zimbabwean currency board that issues Zimbabwean dollars against a 100% reserve of South African rand.

As far as I can tell, the $Dimon is e-money, which is one particular kind of digital money. I have two main reasons for this conclusion.

First, according to the EU Directive 2009/110/EC, 'electronic money' is defined as 'electronically, including magnetically, stored monetary value as represented by a claim on the issuer which is issued on receipt of funds for the purpose of making payment transactions ... and which is accepted by a natural or legal person other than the electronic money issuer'.

This sounds awfully like saying that, as Bloomberg puts it, the $Dimon is 'a digital coin representing United States dollars held in designated accounts at JPMorgan Chase N.A.' (Levine 2019). It is a bearer instrument (so 'coin' is a reasonable appellation) that entitles the holder to obtain a US dollar from that bank and therefore seems to fall within the EU Directive definition, since entities other than JPMC, albeit customers of JPMC, accept it as payment.*

---

* I pull back from calling JPM Coins 'digital cash' because of this need to establish an account with JPMC in order to hold them.

Second, my good friend Simon Lelieveldt, who knows more about e-money than almost anyone else on Earth, said so.

The $Dimon episode confirmed my view that the trading of digital assets in the form of tokens is one of the most interesting aspects of current developments in cryptocurrency as well as a highly plausible mechanism for implementing robust digital money.

Rethinking the system

Moving towards digital currency gives us an opportunity to rethink some of the existing concepts around money, payments and banking as well as e-cash itself. We can use the arrival of digital currency to catalyse other changes to the IMFS that are desperately needed as it is reshaped to support the new economy. One area that is in particular need of reform is the AML regime.

It does not seem to be working terribly well (*Economist* 2019c). Regulators have fined banks $28 billion for money laundering and sanctions violations over the last decade, and something like $9.5 billion more for aiding tax evaders. As the fines go up, so does bank spending – and the numbers are staggering. At the end of 2018, 15% of Citigroup's 204,000 employees worked in compliance, risk or control functions (whereas a decade ago it was only 4%), and HSBC has 5,000 people working on AML. HSBC and Standard Chartered each spend half a billion dollars per annum on AML, and the Financial Conduct Authority estimates that total AML spending by British banks is now about £5 billion per annum.

Overall, of the estimated $2 trillion that is laundered globally every year, the regtech experts at ComplyAdvantage say that only 1–3% of these funds are identified and possibly stopped. Even if financial services and other businesses had infinite compliance budgets, which they most certainly do not, it is simply not feasible to hire enough people to keep up. And even if there were infinite people with expertise in the space, which there most certainly are not, bringing them on board would be too time consuming, too expensive and too inflexible to create a compliance infrastructure able to respond to the new environment.

Technology is the only way out of this. Using technology to automate current procedures is, as always, only a small part of the solution. According to the National Crime Agency, the UK Financial Intelligence Unit (UKFIU) receives more than 460,000 suspicious activity reports (SARs) every year, yet fraud continues to rise.

Moreover, as Rob Wainwright (head of Europol) pointed out last year, European banks are spending some €20 billion per annum on KYC, AML, CTF and politically exposed person (PEP) monitoring, with very limited results. In fact, he specified that 'professional money launderers – and we have identified 400 at the top, top level in Europe – are running billions of illegal drug and other criminal profits through the banking system with a 99 percent success rate'. This is not the Red Queen's race: it is the Formula 1 of crime, where the bad guys are ahead and we cannot overtake them.

AMLDV, which had to be enacted by EU member states at the beginning of 2020 (Tomac and Lagodzinski 2019), is unlikely to change this criminal calculus. This directive will cost organizations substantially more than its predecessors, and the costs are out of control. According to a 2017 white paper written by my colleagues at Consult Hyperion, KYC processes currently cost the average bank $60 million

(€53 million) annually, with some larger institutions spending up to $500 million (€441 million) every year on KYC itself and associated customer due diligence (CDD) compliance. In the AMLDV era, we will look back with nostalgia at a time when the costs of compliance were so limited.

It is time for a rethink. We need to re-engineer regulators and compliance to stop implementing KYC, AML, CTF and PEP measures by building electronic analogues of passports, suspicious transaction reports and so on. In this world of machine learning and AI, we need to invert the paradigm: instead of using CDD to keep the bad guys out of the system, we should bring the bad guys into the system; use AI, pattern recognition and analytics to find out what the bad guys are doing; and catch them!

Surely, from a law enforcement point of view, it is better to know what the bad guys are up to. Following their money should mean it is easier to detect and infiltrate criminal networks and to generate information that the law enforcement community can use to *do something* about the flow of criminal funds. In any other financial services business, a success rate of 1% would call into question the strategy and the management of the company.

Hence, replacing cash with digital money – even if it is anonymous to certain levels – should be seen as a positive step towards a better regime that will actually do more to help law enforcement.

Chapter 6

Creating digital fiat

Should central banks issue a new digital form of money? A state-backed token, or perhaps an account held directly at the central bank, available to people and firms for retail payments?

— Christine Lagarde, speaking at the
Singapore Fintech Festival (2018)

Why not just do away with bank accounts and have the central bank provide digital currency to everyone? Such a move would have some pretty major ramifications, which is why Lagarde's question is so important. Greg Medcraft, chair of the Australian Securities and Investment Commission, has questioned the status quo quite plainly (Eyers 2017):

> Traditional bank current accounts may disappear in the next decade because central banks will create digital currencies and provide payment accounts to customers directly.

To think about this, we need to be clear about what a CBDC might be in monetary terms. Ulrich Bindseil at the ECB has set out an admirably clear taxonomy in which CBDC could be considered a third form of base money, distinct from both overnight deposits with the central bank (currently available only to banks, specific non-bank financial firms and some official sector depositors) and banknotes. It is a lazy label, but let us call the former case 'wholesale' currency and the latter case 'retail' currency (Bindseil 2020). Wholesale digital currency is not particularly interesting in our context, so let us focus on retail digital currency in the form of central bank money provided to all households and businesses. In other words, CBDC is a universally accessible digital fiat, as shown in figure 10 (Bjerg 2017).

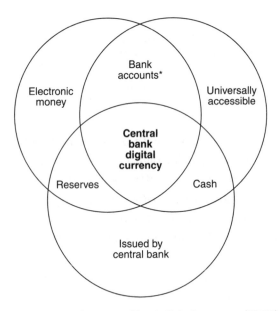

Figure 10. Locating central bank digital currency (CBDC).

No matter how beneficial it might be to society, CBDC has two well-understood problems that are identified in figure 10. The first is that it would disintermediate banks, and the second is that it might destroy banks (because bank deposits

_____

* Yes, I know bank accounts are not, in practice, available to anyone, but that is not important to the discussion.

would be traded for zero-risk central bank money). Central bankers, being naturally somewhat conservative, do not want to either disintermediate or destroy banks in the same way that Bitcoiners do; so, they will look for what are generally called two tier solutions, in which the central bank creates and monitors the digital money but commercial banks manage it.

Thus, while CBDC could be implemented via accounts held directly at the central bank (or at a government-owned bank, such as a postal savings bank), it is more likely to be provided to the public via specially designated accounts at supervised commercial banks or other regulated institutions (e.g. payments institutions in the EU). In the latter case, institutions would hold the corresponding amount of funds in segregated reserve accounts at the central bank, an approach that is sometimes called a synthetic CBDC (Fernández-Villaverde *et al.* 2020), although I prefer to stay with the 'two tier' label. This is no different from the bank-led experiments of the 1990s (Mondex, etc.) but uses new technology. It is difficult in any case to say which might be best without understanding what society actually wants from a CBDC and what characteristics are desirable.

Digital fiat characteristics

We have the motivation we need to move on and create a CBDC. If we return to table 4 (in chapter 3) and focus on the case of a specific CBDC, there are obviously some fundamental central bank concepts around digital money that we need to bear in mind when we design a solution. Ben Dyson and Jack Meaning from the Bank of England have set out a particular kind of digital currency that could be issued by a central bank with quite specific characteristics (which corresponds to what I am calling 'digital fiat' here). This appears to be an excellent starting point. They describe digital fiat that is (Dyson and Meaning 2018):

- universally accessible (anyone can hold it);

- interest-bearing (with a variable rate of interest);

- exchangeable for banknotes and central bank reserves at par (i.e. one-for-one);

- based on accounts linked to real-world identities (not anonymous tokens); and

- withdrawable from bank accounts (in the same way that you can withdraw banknotes).

This seems to me quite a sensible definition: a CBDC is digital fiat that is one particular kind of digital currency, which is one particular kind of digital money. Makes sense.

Some years ago, David Andolfatto, vice president of the Federal Reserve Bank of St. Louis, said that it was 'hard to see the downsides to central banks supplying digital currency' (Andolfatto 2015). I agree, although I have long held the view that central banks will be just one of the providers of digital money – and, as we will see, the battle lines are already being drawn up. However, we are focusing on central bank money, and it is therefore reasonable to ask how digital fiat will work.

We have to start by filling in some blanks. For example, should CBDC be centralized, distributed or decentralized? *The Economist* noted in an article about giving everybody access to central bank money that 'administrative costs should be low, given the no-frills nature of the accounts' (*Economist* 2018). Given that a centralized system has the lowest cost, all signs seem to point towards something like M-Pesa, but a version run by the government, rather than something built using federated databases or decentralized shared ledgers. The World Economic Forum notes that one of the arguments against such an account-based system, and it is a valid concern, is that a system like this presents more of a challenge to existing commercial banks' business models, whereas the kind of token-based alternatives I envisage are more of a cash replacement (World Economic Forum 2020).

Either way, the shift towards digital fiat will restructure the financial system, and therefore it needs careful planning. If people start using digital fiat instead of banknotes and move money from their (to a certain extent risk-free) bank accounts to their central bank digital fiat balances, then this could set in motion a disintermediation of the banking sector as a whole. This is why economists distinguish between digital fiat that substitutes for banknotes and digital fiat that substitutes for bank deposits. As you can see from figure 11, bank deposits account for almost half of bank funding requirements in the eurozone, and at low cost. If you take these away, you have to have a plan for the banks.

As Lael Brainard, a member of the Board of Governors of the Federal Reserve, pointed out in an October 2019 speech, population-scale public or private digital currencies challenge current commercial bank business models and could both disintermediate the role of banks in payments and affect their sources of funds (Brainard 2019). Moreover, the widespread use of such currencies would reduce the visibility of transactions data for banks, thereby hindering their ability to price risk. This is an issue that has long been recognized in China, where the rise of non-bank mobile app payments at the expense of credit and debit cards has restricted commercial banks' access to customer data: access that is crucial to emerging business models (Wildau 2016).

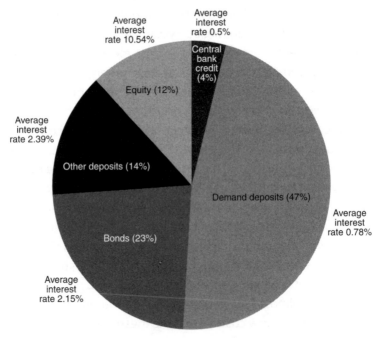

Figure 11. Cost of bank funding in Europe.

When we are discussing the impact of digital currency later in this book, I will be assuming that we are talking about 'greater' digital fiat, which will provide a risk-free substitute for commercial bank deposits. The ECB modelling of this kind of digital fiat, in comparison with a stablecoin currency board or a commercial bank digital currency, seems to indicate that the business case for what I have labelled the two tier* digital currency is at least plausible. That is, digital fiat is managed by the central bank on the basis of commercial bank deposits, and people (and businesses) get the digital fiat from the commercial banks.

Retail currency

Now, bearing these issues in mind and remembering the differences between cryptocurrency and digital currency, let us review a few of the key issues with creating a digital fiat currency.

- A monetary regime with central bank-issued national digital currency (i.e. digital fiat) has never existed anywhere, a major reason being that the technology to make it feasible and resilient has been unavailable until now. Since we have the technology, and we should use it, we need to design our new system from first principles (rather than by emulating the money we have now).

- The monetary aspect of private digital currencies (i.e. having a competing currency with an exogenous predetermined money supply) may be seen as undesirable from the perspective of policymakers, even if it might be advantageous to individuals and to businesses.

- The move to digital fiat means the central bank will have to grant universal, electronic, 24/7 national currency denominated and interest-bearing access to its balance sheet.

---

* Please note that this is not what the ECB means by two tier; I am sticking to my usage here.

- The cheapest alternative to running such a system would be a fully centralized architecture like M-Pesa. To some observers, simply giving anyone and everyone an account at the central bank is the cheapest and simplest way forward. Supporters of that approach see this kind of 'direct' central banking as more effective, saving-friendly and consumer-friendly than the current 'indirect' approach (Hockett 2019a).

- Costs to one side, there may be other reasons for wanting to use some form of shared ledger implementation instead (e.g. resilience). One feature of such a shared ledger system is that the entire history of transactions is available to all verifiers, and potentially to the public, in real time. It would therefore give policymakers a great deal more data as well as the ability to observe the response of the economy to shocks and policy changes almost immediately.

Of course, should we in post-Brexit Britain decide to create a British CBDC issued and managed by commercial banks (let us call it Brit-Pesa), we would not use either the smart cards of the Mondex days or the basic SIM toolkit and SMS technology of M-Pesa. We would use smartphones, chatbots, AI, fingerprints, voice recognition and all that jazz (the biometrics, blockchains and bots we discussed in chapter 2).

I do not think it would be that difficult or that complicated to create a basic centralized CBDC: a system shared by the commercial banks with funds held in a central account. Whether digital fiat is the long-term future of money or not (and I think not), on balance I believe the United Kingdom should get on with CBDC – whether in the form of Brit-Pesa, Brit-Ledger or Brit-Dex – and give everyone access to payment accounts without credit risk. Aside from forging a new financial system in the white heat of new technology, there is a very good reason for doing this. A Bank of England working paper on the topic says (among other things) that (Barrdear and Kumhof 2016):

> We find that CBDC issuance of 30% of GDP, against government bonds, could permanently raise GDP by as much as 3%, due to reductions in real interest rates, distortionary taxes, and monetary transaction costs. Countercyclical CBDC price or quantity rules, as a second monetary policy instrument, could substantially improve the central bank's ability to stabilize the business cycle.

GDP growth aside, there is another excellent reason to take this step: cash has no API. Writing for the Bank of England's *Bank Underground* blog, Simon Scorer from the central bank's digital currencies division made a number of very interesting points about our need for some form of digital fiat (Scorer 2017). He remarked on the transition from dumb money to smart money and the consequent potential for the implementation of digital fiat to become a platform for innovation (something I strongly agree with). Scorer explained:

> Other possible areas of innovation relate to the potential programmability of payments; for instance, it might be possible to automate some tax payments (e.g. when buying a coffee, the net amount could be paid directly to the coffee shop, with a 20% VAT payment routed directly to HMRC),[*] or parents may be able to set limits on their children's spending or restrict them to trusted stores or websites.

---

[*] Her Majesty's Revenue and Customs.

If digital fiat were to be managed via some form of shared ledger, then Scorer's insights here suggest that it is not the shared ledger but the shared ledger applications (smart contracts) that will become the nexus for radical innovation, as they are what we shall use to implement new digital currencies.

Brit-Coin or Brit-Pesa?

Back to the central design choice that we need to make, then, and to Lagarde's speech, which I quoted in the opening of this chapter (Lagarde 2018):

> Should central banks issue a new digital form of money? A state-backed token, or perhaps an account held directly at the central bank, available to people and firms for retail payments?

This is the question we need to tackle first in the design of a digital replacement for fiat currency: in other words, Brit-Ledger, Brit-Coin or Brit-Dex? The IMF's Staff Discussion Note 18/08 on which Lagarde's speech is based sets out the two options of token-based or account-based CBDC very clearly.

A token-based CBDC – with payments that involve the transfer of an object (namely, a digital token) – could extend some of the attributes of cash to the digital world. CBDC could provide varying degrees of anonymity and immediate settlement. It could thus curtail the development of private forms of anonymous payment but might increase risks to financial integrity. Design features such as size limits on payments in and holdings of CBDC would reduce but not eliminate these concerns.

An account-based CBDC – with payments through the transfer of claims recorded on an account – could increase risks to financial intermediation. It would raise funding costs for deposit-taking institutions and facilitate bank runs during periods of distress. Again, careful design and accompanying policies should limit these risks, but they will not completely erase them. The ECB reckon that introducing this type of CBDC to the eurosystem would mean going from the 10,000 accounts it has now to perhaps half a billion.*

This speech caught my attention because, as you will have deduced from part 1 of this book, I think Lagarde is right to mention state-backed tokens as an option. In this case, digital fiat is simply a particular kind of cryptoasset, which happens to be digital money based on an institutional binding[†] to a 100% reserve in national currency (or currencies, of course).

Now, nothing in the IMF formulation makes the use of tokens (rather than a central database) inevitable. There are, however, other arguments in favour of using the meta-technology of digital money to build more sophisticated versions of cash: the very smart money discussed earlier. One of them is privacy. In that same speech, Lagarde said:

> Central banks might design digital currency so that users' identities would be authenticated through customer due diligence procedures and transactions recorded. But identities would not be disclosed to third parties or governments unless required by law.

As a fan of practical pseudonymity as a means of raising the bar on both privacy and security, I am very much in favour of exploring this line of thinking. Technology gives us ways both

* Why this speech was reported in some outlets as being somewhat supportive of cryptocurrencies is puzzling, especially since Lagarde specifically says in it that she remains unconvinced about the 'trust = technology' – that is, the 'code is law' – view of cryptocurrencies.
† Where the institution is the central bank.

to deliver appropriate levels of privacy into this kind of transactional system and to do it securely and efficiently within a democratic framework. In particular, new cryptographic technology offers us the apparently paradoxical ability to keep private data on a public ledger, which I think will form the basis of new financial institutions that work in new kinds of markets (e.g. the 'glass bank' I am so fond of using as a key image). So, let us tackle this privacy issue head on.

An elephant in the room

If there is to be a digital fiat, then it will have a cultural context. As *The Economist* has noted, people might well be 'uncomfortable with accounts that give governments detailed information about transactions, particularly if they hasten the decline of good old anonymous cash'. This anonymity is a feature of physical cash that payment cards and instant credit transfers do not have, and some observers see it as a freedom that is being taken away (Orcutt 2020). To replicate bearer instruments such as notes and coins – to have a form of money that we *can* use in transactions with other people without a third party getting in the way, that surveillance capitalists *cannot* use to build advertising profiles, and that governments *cannot* use to track our spending or our movements – we need to be clever about the technology we put in place.

However, as I set out in my book *Identity Is the New Money*, there are ways to deliver the appropriate levels of privacy into this kind of transactional system: pseudonymity is an obvious way to do this efficiently within a democratic framework. Thus, while we could envisage digital fiat as M-Pesa run by the central bank or a sort of government PayPal, there are arguments in favour of using newer and more radical meta-technology architecture to deliver a more modern and more sophisticated money infrastructure that provides considerably more privacy and more security than the current electronic payment infrastructure. We have the cryptographic tools (such as the aforementioned zero-knowledge proofs, which are used in systems like Zcash) to deliver both privacy and security, but, as I often comment on this topic, it is for society to decide where to set the dial on these, not technologists.

Privacy by design

J. P. Koning's excellent paper on options for a Brazilian CBDC (Koning 2018) mentions Narayana Kocherlakota, former CEO of the Federal Reserve Bank of Minneapolis, who wrote in 2016 that economists do not know very much about the topic of anonymity and who 'calls for the profession to model it more systematically'. I think this is a really critical point. The optimum anonymity level of cash replacement products should be discussed in the context of implementing a digital fiat currency of one form or another. Koning's paper explores three ways to implement a CBDC for Brazil, each of which illustrates the design choices that need to be made should we go down this route. The options discussed are as follows.

- MoedaElectronico (ElectronicCash): this is the most cash-like of the three CBDCs. It neither pays positive interest nor docks negative interest, and it is anonymous. Like cash, it is a bearer token.

- ContaBCB (BCBAccounts): this is the most account-based of the three templates. Accounts are non-anonymous and pay interest, like normal bank accounts.

- MoedaHíbrida (Hybridcash): this provides a mix of cash and account-like features, including the ability to pay a varying positive and negative interest rate, while offering users a choice between anonymity and no anonymity.

The first two are well known and well understood, but let us look at that third example in more detail. Koning says that the case can also be made for a permanently negative interest rate on an anonymous CBDC. Why? Well, since we all understand that criminality and tax evasion impose costs on society, it may be worthwhile designing anonymous payment systems in a way that recoups some of the costs that these activities impose.

In other words, we can use the meta-technology to construct a cash replacement system in which anonymous transactions cost more than non-anonymous transactions. One way to do this, which is referenced by Koning, is with the 'light and dark' CPS we discussed earlier, implemented using Zcash and a mechanism of shielded and unshielded transactions as the basis for MoedaHíbrida's two different modes. If the user decides to hold shielded (i.e. dark) MoedaHíbrida tokens, then all transactions made with those tokens are completely anonymous and untrackable. However, should the user decide to hold unshielded (i.e. light) MoedaHíbrida tokens, all transactions can be seen.

Offering people the choice of anonymity but making them pay for it is a radical solution, but it deserves attention. What I think is very clever about using negative interest rates instead of fees (which never occurred to me) is that it allows for anonymous transactions without imposing transaction friction, thus providing a cash substitute in the marketplace while penalizing those who stash anonymous cash. The negative interest rate means that dark tokens will be subject to a negative interest rate of, say, −5% per annum, while light tokens will receive a competitive interest rate.

Whether or not this is the way forward, it is a line of thought that deserves serious examination in the context of CBDC design. If it is considered important to society to provide anonymous means of exchange, then having a 'tax' on the anonymous store of value seems a reasonable way to distribute the costs and benefits for society as whole.

A thought experiment: MacPesa

Let us put together some ideas using the meta-technology and the drivers discussed so far to explore how a digital currency might come to pass and what it might look like. I will use a topical post-Brexit example that we can have some fun with: Scotland.

Scotland already has its own sort of currency board, as Scottish banknotes are issued against sterling deposits at the Bank of England. These are not without their problems abroad, though. Consider the recent example of a British police force who launched an investigation after a man complained that a branch of the Post Office in England would not accept his Scottish banknotes. This incident was entered into UK official statistics as a hate crime.

Never mind the Post Office: no one anywhere need accept Scottish banknotes for anything. For one, Scottish banknotes are not legal tender anywhere, even in Scotland (Scottish law, which is separate from the law of England and Wales, has no concept of legal tender). So, the Post Office is no more obliged to accept a Scottish fiver than it is to accept euros, gold or cowrie shells. The story did, however, cause me to reflect on what will happen if, post-Brexit, Scotland votes to leave the United Kingdom. Will Scotland then join the euro or create its own currency?

As supporters of Scottish independence insist, once Scotland becomes an independent country, it will be responsible for managing its own currency in the same way as every other country that has its own currency. But how should the Scots go about creating this currency? Surely messing around with notes and coins, other than for post-functional symbolic purposes, is a total waste of time – and money?

A much better idea would be to go straight to the modern age and create MacPesa: this would be a digital money system rather like Kenya's M-Pesa (as discussed in the earlier case study), with a few crucial enhancements to take advantage of new technology. M-Pesa is an amazing success, but it is not perfect. In recent times, it has gone down, leaving millions of customers unable to receive or send money. These failures cost the economy a significant amount (billions of shillings), which is not surprising when you remember that M-Pesa moves billions of Kenyan shillings every day. So, when M-Pesa drops out, it leaves customers hanging, it leaves agents losing revenue and it leaves the banks unable to transact.

It is now a vital piece of national infrastructure, just as MacPesa would be.

I have indicated that the M-Pesa system goes down from time to time; so, what if there were no system in the middle to go down anymore? What if the TELCOs, regulators and banks were to cooperate on some form of ESL– a commercial-grade shared ledger solution, where the nodes all have a copy of the ledger and take part in a consensus process to commit transactions to that ledger – in order to implement an IMF-style token-based solution? Could it work?

Let us do the math, as our American cousins say. Suppose there are 10,000 agents across Scotland with 100 'super agents' (network aggregators) managing 100 agents each. Suppose that there are 10 million customers (there are currently around 20 million in Kenya, which has 10 times the population of Scotland). Suppose also that a customer's MacPesa balance and associated flags/status is 100 bytes.

So, 100 bytes × 10 million customers is 1,000,000,000 bytes, which is 1 gigabyte. My iPhone stores 256 gigabytes. A gigabyte is nothing.

You can have a 24/7, 365 scheme without having a MacPesa system in the middle. When you make a transaction with your handset, it gets routed to a super agent, who decrements your balance, increments your payee's balance and then transmits the new balances (all digitally signed, of course) to other super agents. You might even imagine, thanks to the miracles of homomorphic encryption, that every agent's node will store every customer's balance without actually being able to read those balances.

So, when Alice wants to send Bob 10 thistles (my name for the currency of an independent Scotland), Alice can connect to any agent node (her phone will have a random list of agents – if it cannot connect to one, it will simply connect to another), which will decrement her encrypted balance by 10 and increment Bob's encrypted balance by 10, then send the transaction off into the network so that everyone's ledger gets updated.*

---

* This is a bit like making an ATM network in which every ATM knows the balance of every debit card and there is no switch or authorization server that might go down. And if an ATM goes down, so what? When it comes back up, it can simply resynchronize itself.

Why bother with this system? Well, it would be money with apps and an API, and I hope that innovators across a newly independent Scotland (and beyond) would use it to create great new products and services as well as to restore Scotland's position (which it held in the eighteenth century) as a hotbed of innovation in banking, financial services and money.

Scottish independence aside, this architecture is one I think central banks will converge on when it comes to the digital currency of the near future: a two tier implementation, where the central bank provides digital currency to nodes (banks), who then interact with retail and business customers. The reason for using some form of shared ledger to implement this system would not be for the censorship resistance prized by the cryptocurrency fundamentalists, but due to the other beneficial characteristics of shared ledger implementations, such as transparency and reliability.

But will central banks be the only institutions to provide the digital currency of the new age? I think not, so it is time to move on and discuss the competition that is just around the corner.

Let us go virtual

A virtual currency made from digital cash denominated in a synthetic unit of account and determined by a basket of currencies does sound a little like Facebook's Libra, which is an example of an ACU for commercial transactions. We will look at Libra in some detail later on, but at this point it is sufficient to note that while Facebook may have been the first Big Tech to try to establish a global digital currency, other similar proposals are sure to follow (Petralia et al. 2019). This is not a bad thing in many people's eyes. The historian Niall Ferguson has stated plainly that 'if America is smart, it will wake up and start competing for dominance in digital payments' (Ferguson 2019). He is concerned about hegemony and argues that a good way for America to rival Chinese initiatives such as Alibaba and Tencent is to support the aforementioned Libra. Right now, Alipay and WeChat wallets store renminbi sent into and out of bank accounts, but as the People's Bank of China (PBoC) has made clear in its recent pronouncements, these wallets will soon store the DCEP, which is a digital cash version of the renminbi. A Chinese digital currency.

This means that we are now fortunate enough to have two examples to help us explore the dynamics of the competition between private asset-backed and public fiat-backed digital currencies: Libra and the digital currency being created by the PBoC. So, let us delve into the details of digital currencies in the real world and look at the competing visions of Libra and the DCEP in order to form some opinions on possible scenarios for a post-Bretton Woods IMFS. Can we identify a likely path through the social, business and technical roadmap for digital currency?

PART 3
THE CURRENCY COLD WAR

The real challenge for the United States isn't Facebook's proposed Libra; it's government-backed digital currencies like the one planned by China.

— Kenneth Rogoff, professor of economics
and public policy at Harvard University
(November 2019)

In the seventeenth century, the Bank of Amsterdam created an innovative financial instrument that was in effect a standing repurchase agreement (repo) facility (Quinn *et al.* 2020). Eligible coins could be sold to the bank and repurchased within six months at an interest rate of 0.25%. Transactions could be rolled over at the same cost. In return for selling coins to the bank, the merchant received two assets: a credit on his bank account and a receipt for the coin. This receipt entitled its holder to repurchase the coins ('redeem the receipt') at the sale price plus appropriate interest.

Such receipts quickly began to circulate as negotiable bearer instruments, while the coins associated with them remained safe in the Bank of Amsterdam's vaults. This arrangement saved on assay and bookkeeping costs. With so many receipts outstanding, merchants wishing to withdraw coins from the bank now found it cheaper to buy a receipt and exercise the redemption option (that is, close out the repo) rather than execute a traditional withdrawal and cart coins around. Consequently, the largely unused right of withdrawal (without a receipt) was abolished sometime around 1685, and bank balances became *de facto* fiat money. Amsterdam's sophisticated financial markets were soon the hub of Europe's credit networks, and the bank's balances functioned as a Europe-wide currency for merchants. Indeed, in the mid-eighteenth century at least seven governments raised loans in the Amsterdam market that were denominated in Dutch currency. These included Russia, the United States and Spain, making the Dutch currency analogous to the US dollar today (Ferguson 2005).

Yet nothing lasts for ever. Dutch florins are, as you will have noted, no longer the Prime currency. We are coming to the end of the current set of global institutional arrangements for money and are about to enter a new era of digital currencies. And, since the Bank of Amsterdam's innovative instrument went from providing a convenient service to merchants to becoming the basis of a global currency, there is no reason to imagine a future innovation will not tread a similar path.

In the current scheme of things (the IMFS), currencies are provided by nation states and supranational institutions. However, in the future, anyone will be able to create a currency. When both Bitcoin maximalists and the governor of the Bank of England are talking about creating new global alternatives to the dollar, something must be going on. While we have spent a fair chunk of part 2 of this book talking about central banks, how their digital currency might replace cash and what the implications of this might be, the future is, perhaps, more about private currencies than public ones.

In his wonderful history of the subject, *The Ascent of Money*, Niall Ferguson wrote that, for democracies at least, the lesson of history is that war does not pay because 'the economic costs of war are always likely to outweigh the benefits of subsequent reparations' (Ferguson 2001). But he was talking about military warfare, not the type of warfare we are facing now; the economics are different. This time we are in a cyberwar.

We have no specific date for when this war broke out, and there is no conceivable Armistice Day on which it might end. As Bruce Schneier puts it, cyberwar is the new normal (Schneier 2018). World War III has already started, but a lot of people have so far failed to notice because it is in cyberspace. It did not begin because computers and communications technologies reached the Pentagon. Far from it. The very first computers were developed to compute ballistic trajectories, and part of my young life was spent trying to work out how to use radio and satellite technologies to keep NATO computers connected after an attack on command and control infrastructure. In those far-off days, however, the reason for knocking out an enemy's IT infrastructure was so that you could send in your tank columns or paratroopers. There were cyber aspects to war, but that was it. Now we are in a cyberwar and, in Ferguson's terms, it is a war between networks (Ferguson 2017).*

---

* This could make the war movies of the future rather dull. No more *Dunkirk* or *Saving Private Ryan*, no more *The Dam Busters* or *Enemy at the Gates*. Instead, movies will be about solitary individuals in dimly lit bedsits typing lines of Perl or Solidity while eating tuna out of a can.

The Canadian father of media theory, Marshall McLuhan, saw this coming just as he saw everything else coming. Way back in 1970, when the same Cold War that I fought in was well under way, he observed that 'World War III is a guerrilla information war with no division between military and civilian participation'. If you think this sounds overly dramatic, you are wrong. I think it is perfectly reasonable to frame the current state of cyberspace in these terms, because the foreseeable future is one of continuous cyberattacks from both state and non-state actors. In this era of asymmetric global warfare, we can see just how forward-thinking McLuhan was. For superpower rivals looking to advance their global position, it must be obvious that attacking America's economic hegemony will be far less expensive than attacking its aircraft carriers.

Digital currency may be just one front in the ongoing cyberwar, but it is an important one.

Chapter 7

Private digital currency

Digital currencies issued by Big Tech firms would undoubtedly have some advantages relative to fiat currencies.

— Gita Gopinath, IMF chief economist,
Financial Times (7 January 2020)

It is now a quarter of a century since a pamphlet I picked up at the Centre for the Study of Financial Innovation (CSFI) changed my view on the provision of currencies. It was provocatively titled 'The IBM dollar' and was written by the noted lateral thinker Edward de Bono. His thesis on the future of money, later reprinted in David Boyle's superb collection *The Money Changers* (de Bono 2002), was that technological developments in computers, communications and cryptography (my paraphrasing) would reduce the cost of creating money to the point where it would make sense for private organizations to make their own. In particular, Dr de Bono suggested that it would make economic sense for companies to issue their own currency rather than use equities (hence the title of his pamphlet). He went on to say he looked forward to a time when 'the successors to Bill Gates will have put the successors to Alan Greenspan out of business'.

Dr de Bono was arguing that companies could raise money just as governments do now: by printing it. He put forward the idea of private currency as a claim on products or services produced by the issuer rather than as bank credit. In his formulation, IBM might issue IBM dollars that would not only be redeemable for IBM products and services, but also (in practice) be tradable for other companies' monies or other assets. To make such a scheme work, IBM would have to learn how to manage the supply of money to ensure that (due to too many vouchers chasing too few goods) inflation did not destroy the value of its creation. But companies should be able to manage that trick at least as well as governments do, particularly as they have no voters to cope with.

This money would be rather like a corporate bond as a bearer instrument, but with no interest, no clearing and no settlement. A start-up launches, and instead of issuing equity or debt, it issues money that is redeemable against some future service. So, for example, a wind farm start-up might offer money in the form of kilowatt hours that are redeemable five years from now. In the early days, this money would trade at a significant discount to account for the risks inherent in the venture. However, once the wind farm is up and running and producing electricity, the value of the money will rise. There might, in this case, be a demand for renewable energy that drives the value of the money higher than its original face value.

Interest in the concept of privately issued money has been rekindled in the age of 'platform' technology firms such as Facebook. The economists Yang You and Kenneth Rogoff wrote in a recent paper on this topic that unless introducing tradability (which is Libra's plan) creates very significant convenience for users, such platforms can potentially earn higher revenues by keeping tokens non-tradable. Their analysis suggests that if platforms have any comparative advantage in issuing tradable tokens, it comes from other factors (You and

Rogoff 2019). We will speculate on what these other factors might be later in the chapter.*

The issue of tradability is not the focus here, but a key advantage that Big Tech enjoys in such activities is the ability to ensure liquidity and value by guaranteeing its tokens can be redeemed for within-platform purchases, as de Bono imagined. However, You and Rogoff note that the theory of what they refer to as 'redeemable platform currencies' remains underdeveloped. I agree, especially because these platform currencies will be built from smart money that offers new functionality. Nevertheless, one must inevitably wonder if Amazon or Apple could issue tokens that might well displace value from traditional bank accounts. If you are wondering why they might do such a thing, note this comment from a recent National Bureau of Economic Research working paper (Brunnermeier *et al.* 2019) on the idea of private non-bank digital currency issuers creating systems in which consumers hold private money that issuers back with deposits in commercial banks:

> The implications for **data ownership** [my emphasis] are quite different. If consumers hold digital currency exclusively, then the digital currency issuers act as information oligopolists. The banks are unable to monitor transaction data without purchasing it. In fact, digital currency issuers may find it more efficient to set up banks as subsidiaries in order to avoid relinquishing their data.

The business model implied here, in which transaction data is not used to assess creditworthiness or to manage risk, but rather to monitor consumer preferences and behaviours,

---

* Hint: it is not transaction fees.

resonates with much else in the online economy; it will therefore serve to reinforce the push for private currencies.

A system with millions or even tens of millions of private currencies in circulation (some backed by fiat currencies, some backed by claims on corporate assets, some based on access to services, and some based on goodness knows what else), constantly being traded on FX markets, might sound like an unbearably complex situation for anyone trying to pay anyone else. However, as de Bono explains in 'The IBM dollar', in an always-on networked world this complexity is no barrier to trade:

> Pre-agreed algorithms would determine which financial assets were sold by the purchaser of the good or service depending on the value of the transaction. And the supplier of that good or service would know that incoming funds would be allocated to the appropriate combination of assets as prescribed by another pre-agreed algorithm. Eligible assets would be any financial assets for which there were market clearing prices in real time. The same system could match demands and supplies of financial assets, determine prices and make settlements.

Note his adumbration of Bitcoin's lack of intermediaries and settlement. Remember, he was writing this before there was a Google or a Netscape, let alone a PayPal or an M-Pesa. In his vision, you send me an IBM dollar and I put it in my wallet. Instead of bank accounts in conventional fiat currency, companies would hold a basket of such currencies. It is worth emphasizing that de Bono also wrote that the key to any such developments would be the ability of computers 'to communicate in real time to permit instantaneous verification of the creditworthiness of counterparties'. He was thus simultaneously imagining both the pervasiveness of an always-on network and what I term the 'ambient accountability' (Birch *et al.* 2016b) of shared ledger technologies that support the exchange of digital assets (the tokens I discussed earlier).

A viable vision

The marketplace I have described, with tens of millions of such currencies being traded on futures, options and FX markets, might sound unviable because transactions would be unbearably complex for people to deal with. However, as I wrote in a *Financial Times* article several years ago (Birch 2014b), this is not the world that we will be living in. We are not looking at transactions between people but transactions between what Jaron Lanier called 'economic avatars' (Lanier 2013). This is a world of transactions between my virtual me and your virtual you, between the virtual Waitrose and the virtual HMRC: a world in which economic competition across digital networks, and competition between currencies in particular, differs starkly from traditional currency competition. This is because the network externalities that are barriers to competition in the physical world can enhance competition in the virtual world (Brunnermeier *et al.* 2019).

These economic avatars, or bots, will be entirely capable of negotiating between themselves to work out deals using algorithms, as de Bono foresaw. As tokens become a regulated but wholly new kind of digital asset – a cross between corporate paper and a loyalty scheme – they will present an opportunity to remake markets in a new and better way. One might imagine a new version of London's Alternative Investment Market (AIM), where start-ups launch and, instead of issuing money, create claims on their future in the form of tokens. Trading these tokens would be indistinguishable from trading e-cash (because they are bearer instruments with no clearing or settlement), but it would add transparency to corporate affairs because certain aspects of such transactions would be public. Market participants would be able to assess and manage risk, regulators would be able to look for patterns and connections. I would be able to see that your assets exceed your liabilities without necessarily being able to see what those assets or liabilities are.

An IMF paper on the subject illustrates just what a significant change this new technology might deliver, and why, decades after de Bono floated the idea, the financial system might adopt it (Adrian and Mancini-Griffoli 2019). This implementation would not be due to any idealogical or technological fancy, but because the system is cheaper and offers more functionality:

> If assets like stocks and bonds were moved to blockchains, blockchain-based forms of e-money would allow seamless payment of automated transactions (so-called delivery versus payment, assuming blockchains were designed to be interoperable), thereby potentially realizing substantial efficiency gains from avoiding manual back-office tasks.

When they are properly regulated, as I am sure they will be in time, tokens will be a more efficient way to manage such a mass-market solution. There will not be some giant IMF database that manages the new kinds of money. In this market, company perfomance will reward private money holders by improving the exchange rate against other private monies. No coupons or dividends. No clearing or settlement.

No hiding how many tokens you have out there. The cost of trading these tokens will be a fraction of the cost of trading stocks and bonds, which is why liquidity will seep out of existing markets and into these new and more efficient structures. Stephen McKeon, a finance professor at the University of Oregon, summarized this imperative by saying that assets of all kinds will tokenize because they will lose the 'liquidity premium' if they do not.

If that seems a far-fetched view of the future, let me quote from a white paper produced by the conservative Swiss payment organization SIX (Dahinden *et al.* 2019). In its analysis of the future of money scenarios, it has one called 'moneyless' (which it incorrectly labels as 'medium to low probability'), where

> the 'price' of any asset can be displayed in real-time in terms of any other asset. Algorithms scout the most liquid pairs of assets to form a *chain of bilateral exchange rates* linking the to-be-priced assets with the to-be-priced-in asset. *Market makers* furthermore provide liquid bilateral exchange rates between different pairs of assets.

This was precisely de Bono's argument. Reading this white paper reminded me that the reason his CSFI pamphlet stopped me in my tracks was that, together with colleagues in the financial and technology sectors, I was already working on systems for decentralized and secure transactions, and I immediately recognized that this was not idle speculation but a vision of the inevitable future.

Now that the combination of mobile phones, social networks and strong authentication has made the necessary calculus cost-effective even for small transactions, the technology needed to deliver the IBM dollar is in place. The world of not only digital money but also digital cash and digital currency is upon us, so we should begin to explore it. In such a world, we can no longer assume that currency will be provided by the nation state through a central bank. The low cost and wide availability of relevant technologies means there is a variety of public and private alternatives.

Ambient accountability

By using biometrics, blockchains and bots to implement very smart money, we end up with an architecture that benefits banks, regulators and customers. We appear to have some promising technology options to deliver those benefits in a way that will meet the requirements of society. This technology has spin-off benefits, too. The use of shared ledgers in financial services – even with no cost benefits and no innovation – will still bring a degree of transparency and accountability to the markets that will have very significant benefits. The cryptocurrency fanatics focus on the uncensorability of permissionless blockchains as the key factor needed to build a digital currency, but I think the technology will be adopted for other reasons.

The transparency and automation associated with having smart contracts, APIs and the ability to constantly monitor ledgers mean that we will no longer need to wait until the end of the reporting period to conduct an audit or to produce its results with the help of skilled financial professionals. Instead, we will find ourselves in an era of ambient accountability, where the technological architecture supports constant verification and validation. It simply will not be possible to write a smart contract that is beyond the bounds of regulation (back to 'code is law')*, and if you want to check whether a bank is solvent before you deposit your life savings there, you will be able to do so by using an app on your smartphone, not by looking at a year-old auditor's report covering figures from many months ago and filtered through many levels of management.

This framework takes us beyond fintech to regtech because the processes of the regulators will be revolutionized as much as the processes of the market participants. Since the regulators will be able to see the state of the ledger at all times, they will be able to spot unusual or inappropriate activity. And since the information stored in the ledgers (albeit in an encrypted form) will have been put there by regulated institutions, then – should there be a need to investigate particular transactions because of, for example, criminal activity – law enforcement agencies will be able to ask the relevant institutions to provide the necessary keys to decrypt specific transactions.

The term 'ambient accountability' is one borrowed from architecture. It describes perfectly how the replicated, decentralized shared ledger will transform the financial services industry. It also serves as a rallying cry for the next generation of financial services technology innovators, giving them a focus and a raison d'être beyond shifting private profits from banks to technology companies and other third parties.

Translucent transactions

Having a combination of fintech and regtech advantages means that a shared ledger can provide more efficient and

---

* In Ethereum's decentralized autonomous organization (DAO) case study, it was possible to write and deploy a smart contract that turned out to be exploitable by attackers. This is because Ethereum is a permissionless platform with no intrinsically defined 'control layer'.

more effective ways to manage a financial services market-place. It provides the right solution to problems that banks actually have. We must, however, note one important and practical implication of sharing transaction details. Some of the information in the ledger is confidential: it can only be accessed by a particular customer, the bank(s) involved in the transaction, and the market where the transactions take place. There are many applications where the transactions must be private. Therefore, we need mechanisms to exploit the beneficial transparency of the shared ledger in such a way that the necessary privacy is preserved. We use the term 'translucent' to illustrate the case where observers can look through a list of bank deposits and loans to check whether a bank is solvent but where they cannot see who those depos-itors are (although they will want third-party verification that they exist!). This is why further development is needed to deliver publicly verifiable private records on such a ledger.

Does the technology for translucent transactions exist? I think it does. In the early 1980s, Eric Hughes – the author of 'A cypherpunk's manifesto' – wrote about 'encrypted open books': a topic that now seems fantastically prescient. His idea was to develop cryptographic techniques so that you could perform certain kinds of public operations on private data; in other words, so that you could build 'glass organ-izations' where anyone could run software to check your accounts without being able to read every item of data in them (Birch et al. 2016a). Nick Szabo later referred back to the same concepts when talking about the specific issue of auditing (Szabo 1997).

I can see that for financial markets this kind of controlled transparency will be a competitive advantage for both permissioned and permissionless ledgers; as an investor, customer or citizen, I would trust these organizations far more than 'closed' ones. Why wait for quarterly filings to see how a public company is doing when you could go on the web at any time to see their sales ledger? Why rely on management's assurances of cost control when you can see how their purchase ledger is looking (without necessarily seeing what they are buying or who they are buying it from)?

A market built up of glass organizations trading with each other, serving their customers and working with regulators in entirely new ways is a very attractive prospect. It suggests to us that new financial market infrastructure may be on the horizon, and that the lasting impact of shared ledger technology will not be implementing current banking processes in a new way but creating new kinds of markets and therefore new kinds of institutions.

In the blue corner: Libra

A scheme to implement a private digital currency based on a shared ledger has already been put forward by Facebook. And, because it is being put forward by Facebook, it is a big deal. A really big deal. Mark Zuckerberg once observed that 'in a lot of ways, Facebook is more like a government than a traditional company' (Conway 2019). Indeed it is, and perhaps it is about to become even more so, thanks to Facebook's plans to introduce a currency of its own. This currency is called Libra, and the media has been full of commentary about both the new blockchain that will support it (created by the Libra Network) and the new wallets that will store it (created by Calibra, a Facebook subsidiary). Here is what Zuckerberg had to say about it during the company's January 2020 earnings call:

We are taking multiple approaches on payments where things like what we're doing with payments and WhatsApp or Facebook Pay overall are built on top of traditional payment infrastructure, whereas the longer-term work that we proposed around Libra, that's now being handled by the independent Libra foundation – we're working on a wallet that will work with Libra. That is more a proposal to make it so that some of the payment infrastructure around the world can be more efficient, especially for things like transferring money across borders.

Putting to one side whether Libra is a currency or not (or a cryptocurrency or not, or a blockchain or not) – a *Central Banking* article said that, as it 'neither [is] a true currency nor bear[s] all the hallmarks of a typical crypto asset, Libra will run on a system similar to a blockchain' (Hinge 2019a) – the fact that it exists is nonetheless exceedingly interesting. This is not necessarily for reasons that are anything to do with money, although it is a payment system of a potentially large scale.

The creators of Libra say they hope to offer services such as 'paying bills with the push of a button, buying a cup of coffee with the scan of a code or riding ... local public transit without needing to carry cash or a metro pass' (Gerard 2019). However, as numerous internet commentators have pointed out, if you live in London, Nairobi, Beijing or Sydney, you can already do all of these things. It is only in San Francisco that a world where people do not write cheques to pay their rent and can ride the bus without a pocket full of quarters constitutes an incredible vision of the future.

From a payments perspective, Libra seems a little underwhelming, although my personal opinion is that having a frictionless Facebook payment system will be beneficial. The ability to send money using the internet is clearly useful, and there are all sorts of new products and services that it might support. A currency, however, has more far-reaching implications. As the economist J. P. Koning points out, Libra promises to be more than a means of exchange (Koning 2019). Libra will be similar to other ACUs, such as SDRs and ECUs, albeit with the potential addition of tier 1 capital to its basket of assets. Clearly Libra is not a digital fiat currency as previously described; nonetheless, it should in theory (unlike cryptocurrencies such as Bitcoin) provide a reasonably stable currency for international trade.*

Table 9. The Libra basket.

CURRENCY	ISO 4217	WEIGHT
US dollar	USD	50%
Euro	EUR	18%
Singapore dollar	SGD	7%
Japanese yen	JPY	14%
Pound sterling	GBP	11%

So, what is the difference between holding Facebucks (as I cannot resist calling them) and holding a 'public' synthetic currency, such as eSDRs? Well, for one thing, the Facebuck currency board basket will not include yuan. In response to questions from a German legislator, Facebook has said that its basket will be based on the US dollar, euro, Singapore dollar, Japanese yen and sterling, as shown in table 9.

---

* Note that, given my 5Cs taxonomy of the future of money in table 4, I would classify Libra as a community currency rather than a corporate currency.

The obvious comparison is with the SDR basket (shown in table 8). The clear difference between the two is that the Libra basket does not include Chinese currency. The composition of its basket aside, though, a key implication of the magnitude of the proposed currency is that, should Libra become the world's transaction currency, its reserve would become a major IMFS player (if not *the* major player). In addition, as former banker Frances Coppola points out, the Libra Association would have the power to allow or deny people, organizations and perhaps even governments the right to transact (Coppola 2019). This is a power most of us would prefer to see reserved for organizations under democratic control. It would be a new and unfamiliar world should the Libra Association be able to create and control sanctions just as debilitating to their targets as those set by the EU, the IMF or the Office of Foreign Assets Control (OFAC).

With its more than two billion consumers who are frequent users of Facebook and its partners' properties, the Libra Association could become in essence a parallel IMFS. While it would still depend on fiat currencies to keep it stable, as Coppola highlights, this does not mean central banks could control it, because buying and selling assets to keep Libra's value stable would be at a scale to move markets. This could influence government policy, as attempts to control Libra might result in the reserve dumping a currency. After all, Singapore's sovereign wealth fund (the money sitting behind the Singapore dollar) is less than half a trillion dollars. Alipay (which may itself become one of a handful of global trillion dollar companies) and Tencent are sitting on 150 billion dollars to service a billion people; Libra is targeting more than twice that many.

There are further significant implications. What if, for example, the inhabitants of some countries abandoned their failing inflationary fiat currency and began to use Libra instead? The ability of central banks to manage the economy would then surely be subverted, and this would almost certainly have political implications. This has not gone unnoticed by the people who understand such things: Mark Carney, for example, has said that if Libra does become successful, then 'it would instantly become systemic and [would] have to be subject to the highest standards of regulation' (Giles 2019). Unsurprisingly, both the international Financial Stability Board and the United Kingdom's Financial Conduct Authority have said they will not allow the world's largest social network to launch its planned digital currency without 'close scrutiny' (Stacey and Binham 2019).

Global regulators have responded to Libra with varying degrees of scepticism. Some jurisdictions (e.g. France) have said flat out that they will block it, although it is not clear to me how. As far as I understand, Libra is a form of e-money that is already allowed in Europe under the provisions of the existing ELMI licences. While the Libra Association remains firm that the system will go live in 2020, many industry observers are already saying that it may never launch in its current form. At the end of 2019, for instance, Swiss Minister of Finance (and outgoing president) Ulrich Maurer was reported by Reuters as saying: 'I don't think [Libra has a chance in its current form], because central banks will not accept the basket of currencies underpinning it'.

However, while there are all kinds of reasons to be sceptical about whether it will reach any of the goals set out by its founders, there is something else that is interesting about Libra.

Using the model I set out earlier to help us understand what the likely trajectory of digital assets will be, let us look at the two institutional bindings needed to turn the cryptocurrency technology layer into a new financial system. These are, as noted, the binding of wallets to real-word entities and the binding of cryptocurrency values to real-world assets. The binding of a wallet address to an actual person is difficult and costly. Calibra says it will ensure compliance with AML/CTF requirements and best practices when it comes to identifying Calibra customers (KYC requirements) by taking the following steps, which I reproduce here in full.

- Require ID verification (documentary and non-documentary).

- Conduct due diligence on customers commensurate with their risk profile.

- Apply the latest technologies and techniques, such as machine learning, to enhance our KYC and AML/CTF programme.

- Report suspicious activity to designated jurisdictional authorities.

So, if we put what the Libra white paper says together with what Calibra says about its wallet, we get a specific version of the model I set out earlier (shown in figure 4). I think it describes the overall proposition quite well.

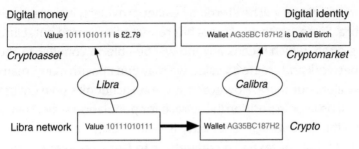

Figure 12. Libra and Calibra in context.

It is noticeable that the members of the Libra Association, launched in October 2019, do not include most of the payment organizations identified in initial discussions (e.g. PayPal and Visa). However, some large organizations that are users of payments (e.g. Shopify, Uber and Spotify) are included.

The head of Libra, Facebook's David Marcus, has recently said that Libra may not use SHCs at all, opting for digital fiat currencies instead, in which case it would become a fairly standard (although large-scale) e-money institution in European terms.

The identity play

On page 9 of the Libra white paper, just at the very end, its creators say that 'an additional goal of the association is to develop and promote an *open identity standard* [my emphasis]. We believe that a decentralized and portable digital identity is a prerequisite to financial inclusion and competition' (Libra Association 2019).

It is clear that any wallet addresses in a transaction (as shown in figure 12), timestamps and transaction amounts will be public because they are on a shared ledger; but as Facebook has made clear, any KYC/AML (i.e. the binding shown in my diagram) will be stored by wallet providers, including Calibra. Since, as David Marcus has repeatedly pointed out, Libra is open, which means anyone will be able to connect to the network and create a wallet, we may end up with many, many wallets out there. However, I suspect Facebook's own Calibra will be in pole position in the race for population scale. Hence, Calibra's approach to identity is really, really important, and its global context as a competitor to (for example) Alipay is becoming clear.

Now, if Calibra provides a standard way to convert a variety of government-issued IDs into a standard, interoperable ID, then it will be of great value. Lots of other entities (e.g. banks) may well want to use the same standard. In the United Kingdom, for example, this would be a way of delivering the proposed digital identity unit (DIU). This was set out in a 2020 speech as part of London's *Identity Week* conferences by Minister for Implementation Oliver Dowden, who described it as 'one login for your state pension and your savings account'.

Yet it is not only the ID that needs interoperability, but the credentials that go with it. This is how you build a reputation economy. Your Calibra wallet can store your 'IS OVER 18' credential, your Uber rating and your airline loyalty card in such a way as to make them useful. Now, if you want to register for a dating site, you can log in using Calibra and it will automatically either present the relevant credential or tell you how to get it from a Libra partner (e.g. MasterCard).

It seems to me that this may, in time, turn out to be the most important aspect of the so-called (by me) Facebucks initiative. What if the Calibra wallet turns out to be a crucial asset for many of the world's population, not because it contains money but because it contains identity?

Government issue

Let us return for a moment to that point about government-issued ID. One of the other things that governments do is issue passports as a type of formal identity. If I obtain a Calibra wallet by presenting my passport, that is fine. But suppose I live in a developing country and I have no passport or formal ID of any kind? Well, I think Zuckerberg could make a good argument that your Facebook profile is a more than adequate substitute, especially for the purposes of law enforcement. After all, Facebook knows who you message, who is in your WhatsApp address book, who you hang out with, where you go … Facebook can even tell real profiles from fake ones: it kills off fake 'identities' all the time. Frankly, in large parts of the world, KYC could be replaced by Known-bY-Zuck (KYZ), to the great benefit of society as a whole.

My guess is that if you have had a Facebook profile for a year, say, then that identity should be more than good enough to open an account to hold Libra up to $10,000 or so. There are many ways that this will be beneficial to society as a whole, not least because any Libra transactions will be placed on an immutable shared ledger.

Chapter 8

Public digital currency

While the Chinese proceed on numerous fronts, the United States continues to take its dollar hegemony for granted.

— James Rickards, *Currency Wars* (2012)

It seems to me, and to many other observers, that the key to taking the title of Prime currency away from the US dollar lies in designing and building a market based on a digital sovereign alternative: in essence, turning sovereign debt (bonds) into money that can be passed from person to person. This would be a market designed from the ground up for the express purpose of exceeding the depth and liquidity characteristics of the US Treasury market (Townsend 2018b). It would extend the safety and security of desirable sovereign debt to global citizens.

At least one nation state is already thinking along these lines. Kaspar Korjus, the director of Estonia's e-Residency programme, has already floated the idea of issuing digital asset tokens instead of sovereign bonds. He said that the money raised in the offering could be used to create a fund jointly managed by the government and private companies. This fund would be used to invest in new technologies for the public sector and to invest venture capital into Estonian companies founded by locals and e-Residents. Eventually, Korjus sees the tokens holding value and being used as a payment method for public and private services, both within the country and globally, which would provide a return on investment to initial coin offering participants.

The Estonian example helps us to answer the misleadingly simple question: what is money? Money is something that you can pay your taxes with, of course! If Estonia goes ahead by merging, essentially, currency and bonds into a single, liquid, circulating digital asset, then we will have come full circle, back to the days when government tally sticks were making their way around England.

Italy has been toying with a similar idea, albeit using paper notes instead of cryptographic tokens: so-called mini-BOTs. These are low-denomination bonds with a value of 5, 10, 20, 50 or 100 euros. Claudio Borghi, president of the government's Budget Committee, has called these 'a spare tire, in order to quit the euro in an orderly way' (Paolo 2019) and has proposed that they be used to pay for government services (including, for example, train tickets). Those behind the idea are clear about its purpose – to introduce a parallel currency not run by the ECB – and the path to population-scale usage, which is to accept these mini-BOTS for the payment of taxes.

Silk purses

As the centre of economic gravity shifts east (or, to take a less Anglocentric view of the world, returns to its historic roots), so the trajectory for digital money is likely to be different from what early pioneers might have imagined only a generation ago. Right now there are some 80 countries that are part of China's Belt and Road Initiative (BRI). These include not only Asian countries and many central Asian republics but also African, Caribbean, Eastern and Middle Eastern countries. In other words, around two-thirds of the world's people, responsible for around one-third of global GDP, are now living along the 'new Silk Road'. Historian Peter Frankopan provides a valuable overview of this new world. As with the Silk Roads of the past, there is no specific geographical criterion one needs to meet in order to take part in the initiative; indeed, the maritime aspect of this new Silk Road is intended to extend its parameters of inclusion to the eastern coast of Africa and beyond.

China's President Xi has called the BRI an initiative that could change the world, and many observers agree. The idea that it will bring peace – 'mutual learning will replace clashes and coexistence will replace a sense of superiority' – however, seems a tall order to me (Frankopan 2018). Whether it attains these laudable goals or not, it is important to understand that while it is an initiative led by China for the peoples of central Asia, the revival of the Silk Road is also meant to send a message about China's aspirations and its position on the international stage.

It seems logical to me, especially given my general feeling that the currencies of the future will be more closely related to communities, that a new Silk Road will demand a new silk purse in which to keep a new silk money. The impact of this money will surely not be limited to trade along these new routes. The impact of digital currencies in general might be more important for states seeking to continue to engage in trade in the face of pressures (such as sanctions), where the dominance of the US dollar and other globally acceptable fiat currencies makes large-scale trade in any of those currencies difficult and large-scale trade in any of the cryptocurrencies too risky (if someone steals your Bitcoins, you are never getting them back).

This appears to be a natural step for countries like Iran, which are, as Frankopan notes, 'attuned to the fact that the world is changing'. While I do not yet see any evidence of a coordinated attempt to create an alternative to the global banking network, it is in the very nature of technological innovation to respond to the drivers of change, and in doing so, some kind of global alternative is likely to assemble itself.

In the red corner: the PBoC

With the focus now shifting east, let us switch our attention to what is (in my opinion, and in Niall Ferguson's too, so far as I can tell) the most important current initiative in the world of digital fiat. This is happening in China, where, of course, fiat currency had its roots. When Kublai Khan became emperor in the thirteenth century, he determined that it was a burden to commerce and taxation to have all sorts of currencies in use, ranging from copper 'cash' via iron bars to pearls, salt and specie; so, he decided to implement a new currency. Then, as now, a new and growing economy needed a new kind of money to support trade and therefore prosperity. Khan decided to replace these various forms of cash with a paper currency. A paper currency! Imagine how crazy that must have sounded! Replacing physical, valuable stuff with bits of paper!

Just as Marco Polo and other medieval travellers returned along the Silk Road, breathless with astonishing tales of paper money, so commentators (e.g. me) began tumbling off of flights from Beijing and Shanghai with equally astonishing tales of a land of mobile payments, where paper money is vanishing and consumers pay for everything with smartphones. China is well on the way to becoming a cashless society as it nears the end of its thousand-year experiment with paper money. A significant proportion of the population already rely wholly on mobile payments, carrying no cash at all – much like me when I am heading into London. As figure 13 shows, in China the cash in circulation is steadily falling, whereas in the United States and the eurozone it is steadily rising.*

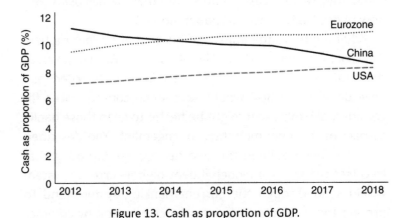

Figure 13. Cash as proportion of GDP.

The PBoC has been looking at a digital currency strategy to replace cash for some years. It now looks as if Facebook's Libra initiative has either stimulated or accelerated the bank's plan. A *Central Banking* article[†] notes that PBoC officials have 'voiced worries that [Libra] could have destabilizing effects on the financial system'. It further states that the bank was planning to 'step up its own efforts to create an e-currency'.

This is no knee-jerk reaction to Libra, though! Some years ago, then-governor of the PBoC Zhou Xiaochuan very clearly

---

* In a recent BBC show on the subject, a UK reporter quoted a rickshaw driver, who turned down cash in favour of a mobile money transfer, as saying: 'We just don't use it any more.'
† See https://bit.ly/2wiCHeU.

set out the bank's thinking about digital currency, saying that 'it is an irresistible trend that paper money will be replaced by new products and new technologies' (Shuo *et al.* 2016). He went on to explain that, as a legal tender, *digital currency should be issued by the central bank*. After noting that he thought it would take a decade or so for digital currency to completely replace cash, Zhou stated that 'he has plans [on] how to gradually phase out paper money'.*

What might be the impact of phasing out paper money? Yao Qian, who founded the Digital Currency Research Lab at the PBoC, wrote on this subject back in 2017. He noted (as I have done) that CBDC would have some consequences for commercial banks, so it might be better to keep those banks as part of the new monetary arrangement. Yao described what has been dubbed the two tier approach, noting that to offset the shock an independent digital currency system would send through the current banking system (and to protect the investments in infrastructure made by commercial banks), one possibility might be to incorporate digital currency wallet attributes into the existing commercial bank account system, 'so that electronic currency and digital currency are managed under the same account' (Knight 2017).

I understand his rationale completely. The Chinese central bank wants the efficiencies that come with having a digital currency but also understands the implications of removing the exorbitant privilege of money creation from the commercial banks. If the commercial banks cannot create money by creating credit, then they can only provide loans from their

---

* As I have written before, I do not think a 'cashless society' means a society in which notes and coins are outlawed, but rather a society in which they are irrelevant. Under this definition, the PBoC could easily achieve this goal for China.

deposits. Imagine if Bitcoin were the only currency in the world. I would still need to borrow a few of them to buy a new car, but since Barclays cannot create them, it must content itself with lending me Bitcoins it has taken in deposit from other people. Fair enough. Here, as in so many other things, China provides a window into the future.

Whether you think CBDC is a good idea or not, you can see that introducing it is a big step, and you can therefore understand the PBoC's position. There is a significant potential problem with digital currency being created by a central bank. If commercial banks lose deposits and the privilege of creating money, then their functionality and role in the economy will be much reduced. We can already see this happening: Alipay and WeChat wallets (and other Chinese third-party payment platforms), for instance, use financial incentives to encourage users to take money out of their bank accounts and temporarily store it on their platforms. It is my observation that, for banks, the loss of interest income will only be a minor inconvenience compared with the much more serious loss of transactional data.

Alipay and WeChat can ease our transition into a world of digital currencies. Libra needs Calibra to create and distribute a wallet to billions of users, whereas Alipay and WeChat already have billions of users for their wallets.

Digital cash is different

A couple of year ago, I wrote that the PBoC was not going to issue cryptocurrencies and that they were not going to issue digital currencies either (at least in the foreseeable future). What I said was that what they *might* do is allow commercial banks to create digital currency under central bank control.

This, indeed, is what seems to be happening. The new Chinese digital currency will be centrally controlled by the PBoC, with commercial banks having to hold reserves at the central bank for assets valued in the digital yuan, exactly as Yao Qian said it would back in 2017 (Leng 2019).

How will this work? Well, you could have the central bank provide commercial banks with some sort of cryptographic doodah that would allow them to swap e-money for digital currency under the control of the central bank. That, of course, brings us back to Mondex.

This two tier approach is how Mondex was structured 25 years ago.* There was one big difference between Mondex and the other e-money schemes of the time, which was that Mondex would allow offline transfers, chip-to-chip, without bank (or central bank) intermediation. Would a central bank go for this today? Would it adopt some form of digital cash that can be passed directly from person to person, like Bitcoin, or some form of e-money, like M-Pesa, using hardware rather than proof of work to prevent double-spending?

This is what was being tested in Uruguay, where the central bank ran a six-month pilot scheme with 10,000 users to test both the technology and the concept (Bergara and Ponce 2018). The driver for exploring digital currency in Uruguay was mostly cost. In line with other similar economies, cash costs this country something in the region of 0.6% of GDP (with two-thirds of that cost falling on retailers). So, from 2017 to 2018 the central bank conducted an experiment with an e-Peso involving 10,000 mobile phone users and a system based on authentication via Unstructured Supplementary

---

* If you are unfamiliar with Mondex, I cover it in more detail in my book *Before Babylon, Beyond Bitcoin*.

Service Data (USSD). USSD is a bit like text messaging and has been widely employed in emerging markets for online services using feature phones.

Figure 14. Mondex cards, wallet and key fob from 1995.

The reason this limited pilot scheme attracted attention from digital currency nerds such as yours truly is that it allowed for two kinds of digital transactions: peer-to-peer transfers among final users and peer-to-business payments between final users and registered retail businesses. The peer-to-peer (i.e. mobile wallet-to-mobile wallet) transfers sent electronic banknotes between devices without going through a central system.

The fact that a central bank was prepared to at least experiment with a form of 'mobile Mondex', albeit for low values (in Uruguay, the wallets were limited to the equivalent of $1,000 each), may not seem like a huge deal, but it really is. It would make a significant inroad into the financial exclusion issue that I highlighted in chapter 4 as a key area in which digital currencies could be beneficial. And if the PBoC does indeed implement something along these lines, it would really change the global financial services landscape.

Peer to peer

Why is this peer-to-peer quality so important to digital cash? Because it not only serves to overcome the exclusion inherent in the current system and the surrounding regulatory framework, but also provides – if, indeed, it becomes necessary, in order to displace cash – the core of a better way of dealing with the ills associated with physical money. There are, after all, many examples of groups that are disadvantaged under the current system of AML/CTF and its dependence on identification and monitoring. These include the following (Lowery and Ramachandran 2015).

- **Migrants** who want to send money home, and the families who rely on that money. Remittances services are seeing banking services being denied as banks 'de-risk'.

- **Vulnerable people** in post-disaster or conflict situations, who rely on non-profit organizations (NPOs) to deliver humanitarian assistance. Citizens of all countries rely on such organizations to assist in reducing the incidence of terrorism, but these organizations are also denied services because of de-risking.

- Small to medium-sized **enterprises** in development markets who need access to credit, which is often dependent on vanishing correspondent banking services.

- The **regulators** themselves, perhaps most importantly, who may be losing out because people excluded from e-money services are forced to find other pathways, including third countries with weaker compliance regimes, or to go back to untraceable and unmanageable cash transfers.

There is an argument that allowing people access to anonymous or pseudonymous digital cash, up to certain limits, would in the long run help us fight crime, terrorism and so on.

Anonymous and *anonymous*

Niall Ferguson's characterization of Libra as 'not a true blockchain cryptocurrency, but more like a digital currency in the Chinese style' (Ferguson 2019) is telling. The Chinese are serious, but for all of the talk about a blockchain, they have no intention of launching a cryptocurrency. DCEP will indeed implement the two tier architecture. Commercial banks will have accounts at the central bank and will buy the digital currency at par. Individuals and businesses will open digital wallets provided by commercial banks or other private companies (i.e. Alipay and Tencent). This will mean, as Libra will also mean, scale interoperability. The digital currencies in my bank app, my Alipay app and my WeChat app will be freely exchangeable. I must be able to transfer value from my Alipay app to your WeChat app for the system to be useful. If PBoC cracks this, it will be on the way to being one of the world's most efficient electronic payment infrastructures.

Noting my earlier points about anonymity and pseudonymity, I think there is something even more interesting in the PBoC's plans. A variety of observers have expressed some surprise that the PBoC would allow anonymous peer-to-peer transfers, and they were therefore surprised to see press reports quoting Mu Changchun, the current deputy director of the PBoC's payments department, saying that the proposed Chinese digital currency would have the ability 'to be used without an internet connection [and] would also allow transactions to continue in situations in which communications have broken down, such as an earthquake'. Talking about the DCEP tool itself, Mu said that the functionally will be 'exactly the same as [for] paper money, but it is just a digital form'. He went on to confirm that 'as long as there is a DCEP digital wallet on the mobile phone', and 'as long as the two mobile phones touch each other', no network is needed. Mu remarked that 'even Libra can't do this' (Zhong 2019).

That all seems to suggest the system will allow offline transactions (as Mondex did), which means that value can be transferred from one phone to another via local interfaces such as near-field communication (NFC) or Bluetooth. To understand why Libra cannot do this, note that there are basically two ways to transfer value between devices and keep the system secure against double-spending. You can do it using hardware (i.e. Mondex or the Bank of Canada's MintChip) or you can do it using software. If you opt for the latter, you either need a central database (e.g. DigiCash) or a decentralized alternative (e.g. blockchain). However, no matter which one you choose, you need to be online. I cannot see how one can achieve offline functionality without hardware security.

If you *do* have hardware security and can therefore go offline, this nevertheless takes us back to the question of fungibility. On this point, the PBoC is both clear and, to my mind, somewhat surprising in its views. Mu's statement is explicit (Zhong 2019):

PUBLIC DIGITAL CURRENCY

The public has the need for anonymous payment, but today's payment tools are closely tied to the traditional bank account system ... The central bank's digital currency can solve these problems. It can maintain the attributes and main value characteristics of cash and meet the demands of portability and anonymity.

It is important to note, however, that there are different kinds of anonymity: what the PBoC means by anonymity may be very different from what a Zcash user, for example, means by anonymity. It might be useful to categorize these different kinds of anonymity as unconditional, limited* and conditional anonymity. For this last one, under normal circumstances the parties to a transaction remain hidden, but – under certain conditions (e.g. the double-spending of value) – algorithms will reveal information about counterparties.

Unconditional anonymity means that no parties to a transaction nor any other observer can learn anything about the counterparties from the transaction record. So, if I want to use my digital money to do something illegal, I can do so without concern, because not even a government can throw enough computing power at the transaction system to find out who I am or who I paid. Limited (or 'first party') anonymity means that the counterparties' identities are shielded from each other but not from the operator of the system; this is surely what Yao Qian meant by 'voluntary anonymity at [the] front-end and real name at [the] back-end'.†

* Or 'controlled anonymity' as the PBoC calls it (John 2019).
† You can see his presentation at https://bit.ly/2IVZ4tx.

Table 10. What controllable anonymity means.

	IDENTITY DATA?	TRANSACTION DATA?	DERIVED DATA?
Central Bank	Yes	Yes	Yes
Counterparties	No	Yes	No
Banks	Yes	No	Partial

As we will see in the next chapter, the issue of the anonymity or otherwise of a digital currency is central to many of the policy issues that arise from the use of digital currency. So, it is important that we consider this carefully and adopt implementations that deliver what society wants – not simply what technologists will provide.

Chapter 9

Red versus blue

> While sanctions are a valuable alternative to more severe measures ... it is a mistake to think that they are low-cost. And if they make the business environment too complicated – or unpredictable, or if they excessively interfere with the flow of funds worldwide, financial transactions may begin to move outside of the United States entirely – which could threaten the central role of the US financial system globally, not to mention the effectiveness of our sanctions in the future.
>
> — Jack Lew, US Treasury secretary,
> speaking in Washington, DC (2016)

What could trigger a 'currency cold war' between the various contenders for the US dollar's throne? Might this set off a conflict that a historian like Niall Ferguson is alert to but politicians seemingly are not? One could take the view that currency is war by another means, and therefore the continuous and never-ending cyberwar that is already underway will inevitably extend to digital currency. Or it may be that specific triggers (perhaps a regional conflict) could lead to concerted action that compresses the timescale for 'mobilization'.

One such trigger might be the overuse of sanctions as a form of financial warfare, which may already be prompting America's friends and foes alike to look for alternatives (*Economist* 2020). Recently, President Trump has expanded the use of sanctions to extend America's reach in such a way as to support his administration's America First policy. Adversaries such as China and Russia as well as allies such as Britain and France (who are concerned with order in, and stability throughout, the IMFS) are looking for alternatives to America's financial hegemony, albeit for different reasons.

There have certainly been some shifts in the landscape. Last year, some two-thirds of Russia's goods and services exports were settled in dollars, down from four-fifths six years ago (Russia's president Vladimir Putin has said 'we are not leaving the dollar, the dollar is leaving us'). China had the yuan added to the SDR basket after the global financial crisis (but there are capital controls that limit its usefulness as a Patrician, so the yuan still only makes up a mere 2% of global transaction value). As former American Treasury secretary Jack Lew explained to an audience in Washington (US Department of the Treasury 2016):

> The risk that sanctions overreach will ultimately drive business activity from the US financial system could become more acute if alternatives to the United States as a center of financial activity, and to the US dollar as the world's preeminent reserve currency, assume a larger role in the global financial system.

Lew went on to point out that it is hard to change an IMFS overnight, and there are no current alternatives to the US dollar (or US markets). This does not mean the dollar's Prime role should be taken for granted; America 'should not be surprised' that countries are looking to avoid the United States because of sanctions. In fact, Lew warned quite clearly that 'the more we condition use of the dollar and our financial system on adherence to US foreign policy, the more the risk of migration to other currencies and other financial systems in the medium-term grows'. Sarah Bloom Raskin, a former deputy secretary of the US Treasury, made a similar point more recently (Pavoni 2020). She said that sanctions are restraints on trade that create a whole cascade of costs, not just for bankers but, obviously, for the businesses affected, too. She believes the rapid growth in their use is 'something that has not been promoting resilience'.*

It is obviously the case that countries which rival the United States want to escape the stranglehold of the current set of monetary and institutional arrangements. However, it is important to note that the straw to break the camel's back might be the shift in attitude of America's friends. In her manifesto for 2019–24, Ursula von der Leyen, the new president of the European Commission, said: 'I want to strengthen the international role of the euro'. This statement echoes Mark Carney's comments about the US dollar's unhealthy dominance.

Perhaps the interests of allies and adversaries are – for reasons that are entirely different and completely at odds – at long last combining with new technological possibilities to force change.

War footing

In the 'old days' (by which I mean the days before the internet, of course), there were currency wars, but they involved competitive devaluations by countries seeking to lower their cost structures, to increase exports, to create jobs and to give

---

* Again, I am not making a political comment here; I am just noting that this might not be in the best interests of the United States or its allies.

their economies a boost at the expense of others. This is not the only possible course for a currency war (Rickards 2012). There are far more insidious scenarios in which currencies are used as weapons – and not in a metaphorical sense – to cause economic harm to others. These attacks involve not only states and central banks, but also terrorists, criminals and investment banks using sovereign wealth funds, cyber-attacks, sabotage and covert actions of a kind not discussed around the Davos dinner tables.

States, of course, play a key role. Former IMF chief economist Kenneth Rogoff has said that the competition to (at the very least) reduce the influence of the dollar as Prime currency will come from state-sponsored assets. I think that, at the global scale, he must be correct. I do, however, see a role for private currencies at both Patrician and Plebeian levels, and I believe they will have an impact on Permeated currencies also. It is important to note that this is not necessarily a bad thing for some countries. A very interesting recent paper on this topic concludes with a discussion on (Raskin *et al.* 2019):

> the potential for private digital currencies to improve welfare within an emerging market with a selfish government. In that setting, we demonstrate that a private digital currency not only improves citizen welfare but also encourages local investment and enhances government welfare.

Along the 'belt and road', then, digital currency might be not only acceptable, but also highly beneficial. Looking at the current situation, it is clear that the principal threat to the role of the dollar as Prime currency comes not from

Facebook but from China and President Xi's 'project of the century', the BRI mentioned earlier.

For some emerging markets along the BRI – where Chinese fintech providers and their associated payments systems have a strong presence, and where heavy infrastructure investment is taking place – the arrival of a state-backed digital currency would help to internationalize the renminbi while enhancing its attractiveness as a currency for trading and settlement. As Jennifer Zhu Scott (a fellow at Chatham House) points out, most of the large infrastructure projects along the BRI are under the control of Chinese companies, who, given the choice of either trading with each other through US dollar reserves exchanged in and out of local currency or directly trading Chinese digital currency, will obviously opt for the latter.

If Alipay and WeChat wallets become widely used by the BRI's four billion inhabitants, they may well begin by using their own currencies; but they will pretty soon shift to the digital renmibi if it does indeed offer greater speed and convenience as well as person-to-person transfers. Never mind Chinese infrastructure builders: an average street trader in Africa may soon find it more than a little convenient to order goods from a Chinese partner via WeChat and settle their debts via Alipay. And, if they can settle instantly with their Chinese digital currency (or Libra, or something similar), they may soon find themselves accepting the same in payment.

As Elizabeth Rosenberg, senior fellow at the Center for a New American Security (a bipartisan think tank in Washington, DC), notes, the potential to diminish the role of the US dollar and US financial networks in the global economy is 'meaningful' for China (and the global economy, of course) if China's development includes expanding the reach of its financial services and the internationalization of its currency across the BRI countries (King 2020). This would deliver sufficient scale to provide liquidity, payments and the clearing of those payments within a new ecosystem, beyond the reach of Western financial regulation.

These concerns extend beyond US and European interests. In Japan, there are concerns that the yen might be squeezed between Libra on the one hand and the Chinese digital currency on the other. Indeed, Japanese lawmakers have used the word 'alarm' with reference to this scenario (Kajimoto and Kihara 2020). Japanese Prime Minister Shinzō Abe has said that the government will work with the Bank of Japan to study digital currencies and to find ways of enhancing the yen's convenience as a means of settlement.

The importance of digital currency therefore extends far beyond the narrow issues of payment efficiency or wallet brand and into the wider economy. Hence, it has become a lever in economic competition. The analyst Dan Wang has set the context for this competition in stark terms, saying (Wang 2020):

> China finds it politically intolerable that the US has an at-will ability to cripple major firms like ZTE and Huawei. It's now a matter of national security for China to strengthen every major technological capability. The US responded to the rise of the USSR and Japan by focusing on innovation; it's early days, but so far the US is responding to the technological rise of China mostly by kneecapping its leading firms. So instead of realizing its own Sputnik moment, the US is triggering one in China.

I found Wang's reference to Sputnik rather interesting, since he is not the only observer who is looking at the present economic competition through this lens. Indeed, the race for hegemonic digital currency may be best understood in those terms, with digital currency a key element of national strategy. A couple of years before Wang, American technologist and entrepreneur Erik Townsend wrote that 'de-dollarization is a catalyst leading to a new space race'. He expressed a similar sentiment about the importance of driving technology forward to obtain leadership (Townsend 2018c). J. Christopher Giancarlo, a former chairman of the Commodity Futures Trading Commission who recently co-founded the Digital Dollar Foundation, which advocates for CBDC in the United States, agrees. Speaking at the Crypto Finance Conference St. Moritz in January 2020, he said that the term cold war was a bit 'strong' to describe the disparity between the United States and China (although he had obviously not read this book at the time). However, he did state that the economic rivalry around digital currency was reminiscent of 'the race to land on the moon'.

It seems to me, in common with these observers, that a superpower conflict is coming, with currency at its core. The real fear of some big-picture thinkers is that, if this new cold war breaks out – with Calibra facing off against Alipay on the one hand and, more importantly, CNY facing off against the US dollar on the other – then it might turn out that the US dollar is vulnerable. And, whether private or public, if one or more SHCs obtain Patrician status (so that people begin to hold them as a reserve), the nature of the network effects of, well, networks means that the US dollar's position at the top of the pyramid will become shakier than we ever could have imagined a generation ago. That was when management consultants McKinsey & Company wrote that the dollar's dominance could not be explained by the size of the US economy alone. Instead, they postulated that (Farrell and Lund 2000):

> While the political stability and military might of the US are factors, it is the world-class financial infrastructure behind the US dollar that makes the difference: transparent financial markets, legal system, innovation in financial products and so on.

It is the ability of digital currency to deliver on these factors that makes alternatives to the dollar a reality, hence my focus on transparent transactions, ambient accountability, APIs and apps as much as on reserves.

What if this world-class infrastructure can be built in cyberspace? That would be a pretty big deal, because it would mean that a proportion of the world's financial transactions would stop being dollar denominated and demand for the US dollar would fall. I think the *Wall Street Journal* was right to characterize the imminent future of digital currency as a 'coming currency war' between digital money and the dollar (Michaels and Vigna 2019):

> The US dollar has been the world's dominant currency since the 1920s. But if national digital currencies allow for faster, cheaper money transfers across borders, viable alternatives to the US dollar could emerge, embraced by nations and monetary officials concerned about the dollar's outsize influence on the global economy.

Or, to summarize at a high level, as Jerome Powell, chairman of the Federal Reserve, wrote to US congressman French Hill in November 2019: 'a digital national currency may not offer advantages to the US that it may do to other nations' (Derby 2019).

Network power

Since the attacks on 11 September 2001, the US Department of the Treasury has used the world's reliance on the dollar to turn the global financial system into a machinery of control (Farrell and Newman 2020). The US government saw the potential here before most other countries did, thanks to the fact that so many global networks lay within its reach. One of the most important of these networks was the Society for Worldwide Interbank Financial Telecommunication (SWIFT), headquartered in Belgium and created in the 1970s to make it easier to route transactions through banks around the world. Thus, the number of transactions grew and the dollar clearing system allowed banks to reconcile payments denominated in US dollars, making us all even more dependent on the dollar.

Since most international transactions are ultimately cleared in dollars through New York (via correspondent banks), the system delivers Washington significant additional leverage over the global financial system. The ability to see what transactions are going through SWIFT (and CHIPS*) is incredibly powerful. If America blocks access to these networks, then individuals, institutions and governments could be crippled.

Whether you think it is a good thing or not, the dollar's dominance gives America the ability to use the international payments system as an arm of its foreign policy: a power that,

---

* Clearing House Interbank Payments System.

THE CURRENCY COLD WAR

as Niall Ferguson puts it, other countries have found 'increasingly irksome' (Ferguson 2019). For a current example of just who might be finding this irksome, look at Iraq. The Trump administration warned Iraq against forcing American troops to leave the country, threatening to cut off the Iraqi government's access to its own bank account at the New York Fed* (which can freeze accounts under US sanctions or if it is suspicious that funds could violate US law). The New York Fed does not disclose such figures, but at the end of 2018, it held $3 billion in overnight deposits for Iraq (Talley and Coles 2020).

Wargames

A decade ago, the Pentagon ran a 'wargame' in which there were no bombs or bullets, no F-16s or Fulcrums, no aircraft carriers or commandos. Instead, the tools used in the simulated conflict were currencies, equities, bonds and the most dangerous of weapons: derivatives. In this game, America was threatened by Russian and Chinese economic shock troops storming markets rather than beaches, and in one scenario the US dollar was attacked by a new global currency based on gold (Rickards 2012). So, to the people tasked with thinking about the future of conflict, the idea of a currency cold war is not new.

The Harvard University Institute of Politics recently ran a wargame simulation of a US crisis around digital currency (De 2019). The participants included former senior White House advisers and thought leaders such as former Department of Defense officials and former Treasury secretary Larry

---

* The Federal Reserve of New York provides banking and other financial services to around 250 central banks, governments and other foreign official institutions, so its power is immense.

Summers. The premise of this wargame, set in 2021, was that participants were members of the National Security Council, convened to respond to a threat to the United States following the roll-out of the DCEP. The scenario played out with the digital yuan undermining the dollar's global dominance, with North Korea evading sanctions by using a digital alternative to the global banking system to buy nuclear materials and test new missiles, and with a variety of malicious state and non-state actors looting from SWIFT.

Summers focused on the vulnerabilities of SWIFT as the key issue, saying that, right now, 'we have one network that doesn't work very well'. He suggested the US strategy centre on reinforcing SWIFT rather than developing a CBDC.

However accurate this scenario may or may not be, the virtual money debate is no longer about e-money versus digital cash, hash tables versus smart chips or proof of work versus proof of stake. It is all about global power. As a historian, it is natural for Ferguson to remind us that the countries which have forged the path in financial innovation have led in every other way, too (Ferguson 2019). He cites Renaissance Italy, the Spanish Empire, the Dutch Republic and the British Empire, all the way through to post-1930s America. He goes on to note that once a country loses that financial leadership, it loses its place as a global hegemon. And that has some serious consequences.

Rae Deng, a founding partner of Du Capital in Singapore, talks about the 'digital migration' of the economy, which I think is a nice term. She also observes that a Chinese digital currency could 'further facilitate the internationalization of [the] yuan' and form a parallel ecosystem, running alongside SWIFT (Chen 2019) and carried around the world by the BRI. Perhaps Britain could try to promote BritCoin through a parallel Belt and Braces initiative more in keeping with our national tradition of state planning.

Note the real and serious implication of replacing the existing financial infrastructure with a new infrastructure based on digital bearer instruments. No clearing and settlement will mean no transactions going through the international banking system, and no transactions going through the international banking system will mean that America's ability to deliver soft power through SWIFT will disappear.

Swerving around SWIFT

North Korea is, apparently, developing a digital currency of its own. According to Alejandro Cao de Benós, president of the Korean Friendship Association, the Democratic People's Republic of Korea (DPRK) intends to go down the Facebook route: it is planning to create an asset-backed digital currency rather than a digital fiat currency and then use some sort of blockchain with 'Ethereum-style smart contracts' to conduct business and avoid sanctions.

Why use a blockchain? Well, the regime sees consensus applications as a way of enforcing the deals it makes with foreign counterparties. Since North Korea does not trust the United Nations, it relies on Chinese intermediaries to enforce deals abroad. But sometimes, so sources claim, those intermediaries cheat the North Koreans. Hence, they want to bypass intermediaries altogether by developing a 'token based on something with physical value' (e.g. gold) in order to create a stable mechanism for payments in international trade between the regime and 'other companies/individuals' (although this will not be made available to individuals in the DPRK, who will be stuck using the Korean won).

This is not a new idea, by the way. A couple of years ago, the Venezuelans tried to introduce 'the petro', a digital currency backed by the country's natural resources – diamonds, gas, gold and oil – to beat a 'financial blockade' imposed by the United States and others. I will check the world currency markets later on, but my general sense of the matter is that the petro is yet to replace the Swiss franc as a Patrician currency. This is despite President Nicolás Maduro's decree to the Venezuelan Constitutional Assembly at the beginning of 2020 that the state-owned oil company, PDVSA, would only accept petro for fuel sold to airlines. Nevertheless, the petro may prove useful as an input in other regimes' feasibility studies.

The United States and other countries care whether the North Koreans launch an e-Won that stops them from being cheated in international transactions. As pointed out in the *Financial Times* (Stacey 2019), the United States has a genuine and well-founded concern that – the financial element of US dollar hegemony to one side – foreign countries will increasingly use digital currencies 'such as Facebook's planned Libra coin' to avoid sanctions: the outcome of the wargame discussed earlier. Indeed, this was one of the arguments Libra's David Marcus put forward. He said, for example, that a Chinese digital currency running on a Chinese permissioned blockchain could mean the potential for 'a whole part of the world [being] completely blocked from US sanctions and protected from US sanctions and having a new digital reserve currency' (*PYMNTS* 2019).

Western regulators could ultimately ban the use of China's digital currency, but that would not stop it from being used in large parts of Africa, Latin America and Asia, which, in turn, could engender some underground demand even in the United States and Europe (Rogoff 2019). Moreover, you can easily imagine that countries will form cryptocurrency unions to regulate currencies and platforms, standardize technology and maintain the stability of viable alternatives to the current system (Zhao 2019).

Sanctions busters

Sanctions are a serious thing and an important element of American soft power, even though they might be something of a blunt instrument: *The Economist* recently called them 'financial carpet bombing' (*Economist* 2019a). Recently, they have become a more important element of US policy. The sanctions list run by the OFAC, a division of the Treasury, now has some 7,500 names on it and grew by a fifth in 2019.

Now, obviously, the United States is not alone in imposing sanctions, but American sanctions are of special importance because of the previously noted dominance of the US dollar as a transactional currency. American sanctions are pretty scary: once you are on the list (penalized on the basis of evidence you are not allowed to see, and with no right of appeal), you are in big trouble, because non-US firms will not want to deal with you for fear that they themselves will be penalized. I am not qualified to comment on the politics, but I can imagine that if this extraterritorial punishment continues, then a variety of wealthy foreign individuals and powers will be greatly incentivized to find alternatives to the IMFS.

When it comes to cryptocurrency, the United States is already taking action. An Ethereum developer was recently arrested for violating US sanctions against North Korea. According to the US Department of Justice, one Virgil Griffith was arrested at Los Angeles International Airport and charged with violating the International Emergency Economic Powers

Act (IEEPA) by travelling to North Korea to give a presentation about using cryptocurrency to evade sanctions. As observers pointed out, Griffith may have evolved a sub-optimal communications strategy in connection with his travel plans:

> When you plan on visiting a country to teach them how to evade your government's imposed sanctions, best not to tweet about it.[*]

The Foundation for Defense of Democracies (FDD), a Washington think tank, summarizes the situation quite well in its position paper 'Crypto Rogues' by observing that 'blockchain technology may be the innovation that enables US adversaries for the first time to operate entire economies outside the US-led financial system'. While technically this may be slightly inaccurate (there are ways to create anonymous transactions without a blockchain, but let us take this use of the term to mean 'third-party anonymous digital currency'), it does accurately flag that the widespread availability of decentralized financial services threatens to bypass existing infrastructure. The FDD are surely right to say that 'blockchain sanctions resistance is a long-term strategy for US adversaries'.[†]

In its report, the FDD highlights four scenarios that might lead to a diminution of the greenback's role in international trade and finance.

---

[*] Jameson Lopp (@lopp), 29 November 2019: https://bit.ly/344evYM.
[†] Whether using the blockchain to create an immutable record of sanctions-busting transactions is a good idea or not, I cannot say; but, as a general rule, I am someone who believes in the democratic process, and therefore I would prefer it if sanctions were not so easily evaded – especially when you consider why the sanctions are there in the first place.

In the first scenario, a US adversary convinces other nations to use a **state-based digital currency** to conduct trade in the adversary's major commodity export, such as oil.

In the second scenario, an independent **cryptocurrency** such as Bitcoin gains wide adoption in commerce and becomes more relevant to the global financial system. Then, a US adversary begins to build significant reserves in that cryptocurrency. The state thus uses its holdings to gain more influence in the global financial system.

In the third scenario, while planning to create a state-based digital currency, a US adversary makes progress developing digital currency **wallet infrastructure**. The nation develops a state-based digital wallet system, wherein both citizens and foreigners can hold and trade the digital currency and use it for transactions with domestic companies.

In their final scenario, a US adversary has enough success with **blockchain technology** in its domestic banking system that it exports its platform to other nations to integrate into their financial sectors. Less democratic governments – who have fewer regulatory and legislative hurdles – may be the most likely to accept new financial platforms.

Now, no one imagines that a digital currency by itself will render sanctions ineffective, but these scenarios illustrate just how a digital currency might, in context, undermine US strategy. When the Iranian regime, for example, set up a venture to explore Bitcoin payments with a Swedish start-up, the Swedish banks refused it a bank account because they did not want to become subject to secondary sanctions. There is no doubt, however, that moving transactions outside of the international monetary and financial system could help to make other sanctions-evading tactics more effective.

North Korea

A North Korean digital currency has every chance of succeeding under the stewardship of the Workers' Party of Korea and the divine tutelage of the Supreme Leader, Kim Jong-un. His father, the previous Dear Leader, famous for being the greatest golfer in history, was responsible for an earlier experiment in radical transformation through money. This involved the DPRK falling into chaos after Kim Jong-il's government revalued the currency and restricted trading in the old money (thus wiping out the personal savings of the counter-revolutionary running-dog lackeys of US imperialism).

When the North Korean people were not eating tree bark to stay alive, they must surely have noticed that the revaluation of the unit of account did not make the slightest difference to the supply of and demand for goods and services. It made a difference to the market, though. The revaluation and exchange limits triggered panic, particularly among market traders with substantial hoards of old North Korean won – much of which became worthless. Gresham's Law took immediate effect: the Korean People's won disappeared from the marketplace, and people began to use whatever hard currencies they could get their hands on. The Dear Leader therefore launched an attack on this as well, banning everyone (including foreigners) from using foreign currencies such as euros and US dollars. The authorities started a TV campaign asking good citizens to report anybody using such currencies. I imagine the same will apply to digital dollars or electronic euros.

So, if a North Korean digital currency based on gold or whatever does appear, would it help the regime and others to avoid sanctions? Well, it depends. It is certainly possible to design digital currencies that have the unconditional anonymity that Bitcoin (for example) does not. Perhaps this is what Griffith was explaining to the North Koreans in Pyongyang, although to be honest they could have discovered this for themselves on the internet without too much trouble.

Let us imagine they do indeed create such a beast: a bastard child of Zcash and Quorum. What will happen?

The North Koreans have other options for disruption using digital currency, by the way: see John Cooley's super book on counterfeiting, *Currency Wars: Forging Money to Break Economies*, which is about various attempts to destabilize countries by forging their currencies. He talks a lot about North Korea's 'superdollar' forgeries and the like. Think what the coming version of this might be: not counterfeiting physical money, but creating e-money. I cannot help but wonder whether the shift to digital money for retail and person-to-person payments would make a modern-day Operation Bernhard – Hitler's plan to undermine the British economy by forging £5 notes – easier or harder to pull off?

A recent United Nations report estimates that North Korea has generated some $2 billion for its weapons of mass destruction programmes using 'widespread and increasingly sophisticated' cyberattacks to steal from banks and cryptocurrency exchanges. It makes you nostalgic for the days when hackers were stealing credit card numbers to access porn.

IRAN

The recent economic sanctions imposed by America on Iran have had the effect of shrinking the Iranian economy by some 10–20%, which, naturally, has stimulated the country's interest in cryptocurrencies. Bitcoin is apparently used by both the government and the public there to evade legal barriers.

Iran has a complicated position with regard to cryptocurrency. The government encourages Bitcoin mining, but Bitcoin and all other cryptocurrencies are illegal (and are seen as a threat to capital controls). This means that miners have to sell their cryptocurrency on overseas exchanges. Hence, it is interesting to note that, according to the Iranian news service the *Financial Tribune* (2019), the government is preparing to offer tax breaks to miners. Miners who repatriate their foreign earnings will be eligible for tax exemptions.

Despite the domestic ban, there is no doubt that cryptocurrency is an emerging front in the economic cold war with the United States and its allies. Iran's economy has been hobbled by sanctions, but transactions using an anonymous cryptocurrency could allow Iranians to make international payments while bypassing the American restrictions (Erdbrink 2019), and the benefits of this might outweigh the problems (from the government's perspective) of FX controls.

International regulators are not blind to the opportunities that cryptocurrency affords the regime. Back in 2018, the OFAC added Iranian individuals (and their Bitcoin addresses) to its sanctions list after forensic analysis by the Department of the Treasury showed that more than 7,000 Bitcoin transactions, worth millions of dollars, had been processed by these addresses (Ratna 2020).

In a thought-provoking piece for *Foreign Affairs*, Farrell and Newman (2020) gave a stark warning. They said the United States needs to understand that if it continues to 'weaponize the world's financial and information networks', then it may stimulate counterproductive responses. Hence, America should moderate: in the interests of both stability and its own interests. Otherwise, the punitive use of such networks may 'encourage states to defect to networks beyond Washington's control'. This, as they note, would serve to remove important sources of leverage.

There are already signs that this is no longer a speculative future scenario. At the end of 2019, Iran's President Hassan Rouhani called for the Muslim world to combat 'US economic hegemony' by creating an Islamic IMFS. This would permit trading in local currencies and promote the creation of a digital currency to curb reliance on the US dollar, because sanctions are the 'main tools of domineering hegemony and bullying' other nations (Ng 2019).

One might well imagine an Islamic digital currency with a billion global users; I have certainly heard discussions about such a thing taking place before, although always in the context of a non-interest-bearing digital currency based on gold (i.e. not to destroy the US dollar, as in the wargame discussed earlier, but to provide a stable currency for the global community).

I cannot help but note, by the way, that the Islamic State of Iraq and the Levant (ISIL) began minting a physical gold currency back in 2015, with the intention of providing a circulating means of exchange for the new caliphate. It was meant to replace the paper money being used in ISIL's newly conquered territories: primarily the Syrian pound, the Iraqi dinar and the US dollar. However, it faced real problems obtaining widespread use because of the need to trade across borders, which meant that paper money continued to circulate. Although businesses were required to list prices in gold and silver coins, they were happy to accept payment in paper. A digital currency based on gold and traded via smartphones might be a different proposition, though.

Never mind *Star Wars*

Where does this leave us, then? I can tell you this much: the future of money is not going to be a singular world dollar or a pan-galactic credit, and we will not be living in the money-free utopia of *Star Trek* or exchanging the Patrician space currencies of *Star Wars*. Instead, money will be multiplied and fragmented into a great many currencies, and while there may only be room for a handful of Prime currencies and perhaps a few hundred Patricians, we could see millions of Plebeian currencies being used within communities.

This may sound crazy. After all, it would be much easier if everyone was using the same universal renminbi, right? But money is more than the medium of exchange you hand over in the store: it is something you want to keep for the long term. While one kind of money might be best for Starbucks, another kind might be better for your pension.

We should set ourselves up for a world in which there are hundreds, thousands or even millions of kinds of money. Your phone will show you the price of your latte in London loots, but you will transfer money in California cabbages, Apple apples and San Francisco parking permits. Although this style of diversification feels new, its roots can actually be found in the ancient past. Back then, money was memory: I owe you some corn, you owe the priest a cow, the priest owes me some wine. In a clan, claims on assets were a collective memory: an immutable mental blockchain.

That did not scale, though. Isolated villages became connected, trade moved beyond being purely local, and the growth of towns and cities made it impossible to remember who owed what and to whom. An intermediary was needed.

We took the means for deferred payments (the settlement of debts) and turned them into stores of value that could be traded. These, in turn, became a medium of exchange: asset claims moved from memory to clay tablets to coins.

Today, we are no longer in the clan village of the ancient past or the urban anonymity of the recent past. We are in Marshall McLuhan's 'global village', where the digitization of the world allows us to be connected to everyone, everywhere and all the time. Instead of memory, we have social media, mobile phones and shared ledgers. This is why Weatherford has predicted the intermediary of money will soon no longer be needed: we no longer need to remember.

That may sound radical, but remember that the way money works now – as fiat currencies controlled by central banks – is not a law of nature. It is a particular set of man-made, transient institutional arrangements. For the reasons set out in part 1 of this book, these arrangements are changing. What that change will result in is hard to predict, but we can say for certain that one size does not fit all. Just look at the euro, a currency that was meant to unite several nations but is increasingly causing divisions. Think how difficult it is to maintain monetary policy across so many countries with different economies (e.g. satiating both Germany's strength and supporting Greece's weakness), and then try to imagine a single universal currency. Having the same monetary policy for Spain and Slovakia will be nothing compared with having the same monetary policy for Earth and Alpha Centauri Planet 9.

The money of the global village will not be limited to a few national or supranational central banks. The technologies discussed in part 2 mean that literally anyone can now create money. Communities rather than individuals will become central to money creation, and these currencies will be imbued with the values of the communities that create them. I might choose to save Islamic e-Dinars that are backed by gold. You might choose to save kWh$$$ that are backed by renewable electricity. We will still be able to do business together, because exchanges on our AI smartphones shall make it so.

Who will win the currency wars? The truth is that, after setting down part 3 of this book, I do not know any more than anyone else knows. I *can* say that I doubt Libra is the future of digital currency (many observers have noted that Mark Zuckerberg's 'Vision for 2030', published on Facebook in January 2020, did not mention Libra at all), but it is certainly a catalyst for thinking about the future of digital money. What I am more certain about is that there are some people who are taking the notion of an imminent currency cold war seriously, who have a strategy for the battles to come and a long-term plan to win them. It is not at all clear to me, however, that we (i.e. the West, essentially) do.

Amy Webb, painting a scenario for the middle of this century, speaks of a world where China no longer needs the United States as a trade partner because it has built a network of more than 150 countries that operate under the guiding principles of the Global One China Policy (Webb 2019). These countries have network access and the ability to trade within a stable financial system backed by Beijing, and their citizens are free to move throughout One China countries (provided they have earned a high enough social credit score). She is particularly concerned about AI, saying that 'while China was focused on long-term planning and a national strategy for AI, the United States was instead concerned with devices and dollars', but I think these concerns might similarly be applied to the world of money, payments and finance.

Whichever way you look at it, the coming currency cold war is real and inevitable.

Coda

A call to action

America has weaponised the dollar. In the rich and emerging world, the search is on for an alternative.

— *The Economist*, 18 January (2020)

The current IMFS is not the product of a planned and rational process that was created and managed with a desired goal in mind. It is simply not correct to imagine that smart people worked out what to do and then implemented their plan in an efficient manner. Quite the contrary, in fact: our modern economic system *evolved* (and it is hard to find support for any intelligent design in this instance). The evolutionary process involved innovations, repetitions, failures and dead ends. It meant busts, panics and crashes (Lanchester 2019). A great many observers, even without the pressure of private or public digital currencies, think change is overdue. Perhaps another series of busts, panics and crashes will see us through to a new state, because if the IMFS is an evolving system of punctuated equilibria, then we are drifting far from equilibrium right now. It is not only technologists like me who think this. Deutsche Bank, in their 'Imagine 2030' vision report of December 2019, said:

> The forces that hold the fiat money system together look fragile, particularly decades of low labour costs. Over the next decade,

some of these forces could begin to unravel and demand for alternative currencies, from gold to crypto, could take off.

This book has explored where these alternative public or private currencies might emerge from, without making any judgements as to which might be 'best'. It is certainly the case that the concept of private money has been rejuvenated by technological change and is now viable, particularly in the new world of online platforms. Here, private money issuers will energize their currencies by integrating the functions of money with traditionally separate functions, such as data gathering and social networking services. Whether such currencies will be interoperable or tradable is a topic for speculation, but I think we can already see that in McLuhan's global village the theory of optimal currency areas may need reworking. The importance of virtual communities may lead to an environment in which the digital connections are more important than traditional macroeconomic links. We might well see the establishment of digital currency areas (DCAs) linking currency use to a particular digital network rather than to a specific country (Brunnermeier *et al.* 2019). It is no longer fanciful to talk about the end of public monopoly over money.

Historically, getting money to work properly has been the job of the state. We understand that if money can allow trade between different groups of people (and different generations of people), then it allows common rules to be put into place to increase net welfare (Chadha 2018). This does not mean, however, that state provision of money, Bretton Woods and the dominance of the US dollar are the only, or the best, ways to deliver that benefit across societies.

Nevertheless, there are many reasons why a managed transition to future monetary arrangements, rather than panics, crashes and busts, is desirable. And we are where we are, as they say. While it is hardly for me to suggest a defence strategy for the dollar, in light of comments on the post-Bretton Woods world made by people better qualified than I am, I have a few suggestions about how developed nations as a whole might proceed.

First, digital identity. The United Kingdom (and America and everywhere else, for that matter) should take a leaf out of Facebook's book and create a global digital identity infrastructure for the always-on, always-connected world. We need an infrastructure for cyberspace, and we are beyond the limits of what might efficiently and effectively be built on the legacies of the industrial age (passports and driving licences, utility bills and 'real names'). Digital identity is, to my mind, a much higher priority than digital money.

I do not want to divert into what that might look like (I am, as it happens, writing a book about this), but suffice it to say that, to repeat my mantra, we need a digital identity, not digitized identity, and we need this digital identity to be universal. We do not want one identity system for people that does not interoperate with the identity system for things, and we certainly do not want an identity system for bots that cannot talk to people. We want an identity system that everyone and everything can use, so that I can safely delegate the ability to open my garage door to my car. This simply cannot happen at the moment.

Most importantly, we want a digital identity that is sensitive to the cultural and legal norms of societies. In the West, broadly speaking, we might want to set the dials to provide privacy as well as security.

Second, digital money. We need a global e-money licence along the lines of Europe's existing ELMI licence with passporting. We are already seeing the steady separation of narrow banking, payments and investment banking regulation in Europe, and we should accelerate this separation in order to create a digital money ecosystem that is resilient. Mutual recognition of such a licence between Europe, the United States and elsewhere would, I am sure, put in place a framework for the new system.

We need vigorous competition and innovative competitors capable of challenging the incumbents successfully, and we will never get that if we continue to require companies to obtain banking licences and state money transmitter licences in order to challenge Bank of America or Facebook in payments. While we all agree that the provision of credit should be tightly regulated, as it provides pathways to systemic failure that might blow up the economy, payments are different, especially if there are lots of systems from which to choose.

Third, we need digital diligence: an alternative to the existing vastly expensive KYC/AML regimes that create a defensive moat around the incumbents. To animate digital identity and allow digital money to deliver the benefits we anticipate, a new approach is needed. Now that we have a world full of AI and machine learning, it may work better for the purposes of law enforcement (and society as a whole) to stop using KYC to create financial exclusion. Instead (bearing in mind my suggestions about KYZ!), we should aim for financial inclusion and use modern technology to track and monitor transactions in order to locate criminals and terrorists. It is entirely possible to imagine a 'privacy-first' scheme that erects high KYC barriers with limited tracking, coexisting with a 'security-first' scheme that has low KYC barriers but complete tracking.

Finally, we need to take Mark Carney's idea seriously and create new payment systems using these digital identity, digital money and digital diligence building blocks. These should have one or more SHCs (and why not start with an eSDR or a post-Brexit North Atlantic free-trade florin?), designed with the goals of all of society (not only those of technologists) in mind. The aim must be to make at least one of these globally acceptable and able to satisfy the demand for an alternative to the dollar. If our developed nations do not do this, then someone else will do it and leave us out in the cold.

Glossary

ACU: alternative currency unit
AI: artificial intelligence
AML: Anti-Money Laundering
AMLDV: Anti-Money Laundering Directive
API: application programming interface
BIS: Bank for International Settlements
BRI: Belt and Road Initiative (China)
BSA: Bank Secrecy Act (United States)
CBDC: central bank digital currency
CDD: customer due diligence
CDP: collateralized debt position
CFA: Franc of the Financial Community of Africa
CFSI: Centre for the Study of Financial Innovation
CHIPS: Clearing House Interbank Payment System
CPS: Crime Pays System
CTF: counter-terrorist financing
DCA: digital currency area
DCEP: Digital Currency/Electronic Payment
DeFi: decentralized finance
ECB: European Central Bank
ECU: European Currency Unit
ELMI: Electronic Money Institution
ESL: enterprise shared ledger
FinCEN: Financial Crimes Enforcement Network

FINMA: Financial Market Supervisory Authority
ICO: initial coin offering
IMF: International Monetary Fund
IMFS: International Monetary and Financial System
JPMC: JPMorgan Chase
SHC: synthetic hegemonic currency
HMRC: Her Majesty's Revenue and Customs
KYC: Know Your Customer
KYZ: Known-bY-Zuck
NFC: near-field communication
NCSC: National Cyber Security Centre
NIST: National Institute of Standards and Technology
OFAC: Office of Foreign Assets Control
PBoC: People's Bank of China
PEPSI: Pan-European Payment System Initiative
PIN: personal identification number
Pseudonym: a persistent alias to an identity
PQC: post-quantum cryptography
SDR: special drawing right
SEC: Securities and Exchange Commission
SGA (Saga): a partially collateralized stablecoin
SHC: synthetic hegemonic currency
Sibos: The annual SWIFT banking conference
SIM: subscriber identification module, the chip inside a digital mobile phone that links the device to a user
SMS: short message service (the GSM text message service)
SWIFT: Society for Worldwide Interbank Financial Telecommunications
USSD: Unstructured Supplementary Service Data

Bibliography

Adrian, T., and T. Mancini-Griffoli. 2019. The rise of digital money. Fintech Notes Series, International Monetary Fund, July.

American Banker. 2003. Citigroup to drop its online P2P payments service. *American Banker*, 1 October. (Also available at https://bit.ly/2WUlvYk.)

Andolfatto, D. 2015. Should the Fed issue its own Bitcoin? *Newsweek*, 31 December. URL: http://bit.ly/37u3K3Q (retrieved 12 January 2018).

Applebaum, B. 2011. As plastic reigns, the Treasury slows its printing presses. *New York Times*, 6 July.

Ascheim, J., and Y. Park. 1976. *Artificial Currency Units: The Formation of Functional Currency Areas.* Princeton University Press.

Barrdear, J., and M. Kumhof. 2016. The macroeconomics of central bank issued digital currencies. Staff Working Paper, Bank of England, July.

Bergara, M., and J. Ponce. 2018. Central bank digital currency: the Uruguayan e-Peso case. In *Do We Need Central Bank Digital Currency? Economics, Technology and Institutions*, pp. 82–90. Milan: SUERF/Larcier.

Bindseil, U. 2020. Tiered CBDC and the financial system. Working Paper, European Central Bank, January.

Birch, D. 1998. An experiment in micropayments: we've taken real money! *Financial Times Virtual Finance Report*, June.

Birch, D. 2014a. *Identity Is the New Money*. London Publishing Partnership.

Birch, D. 2014b. When anyone can be a money issuer. *Financial Times Alphaville*, 28 May.

Birch, D. 2017. *Before Babylon, Beyond Bitcoin: From Money that We Understand to Money that Understands Us (Perspectives)*. London Publishing Partnership.

Birch, D., and N. McEvoy. 1996. Downloadsamoney. *DEMOS Quarterly* **8**, 85–93.

Birch, D., and S. Parulava. 2017. Ambient accountability: shared ledger technology and radical transparency for next generation digital financial services. In *Handbook of Blockchain, Digital Finance and Inclusion* (ed. D. Lee and R. Deng), pp. 375–388. London: Elsevier.

Birch, D., R. Brown and S. Parulava. 2016. Towards ambient accountability in financial services: shared ledgers, translucent transactions and the legacy of the great financial crisis. *Payment Strategy and Systems* **10**(2), 118–131.

BIS. 2015. Digital currencies. CPMI Paper, Bank for International Settlements, November.

Bjerg, O. 2017. Designing new money: the policy trilemma of central bank digital currency. Working Paper, Copenhagen Business School, June.

Brainard, L. 2019. Digital currencies, stablecoins and the evolving payments landscape: speech at *The Future of Money in the Digital Age*, sponsored by the Peterson Institute for International Economics and Princeton. Speech 1095, Board of Governors of the Federal Reserve System (US).

Brunnermeier, M., H. James and J.-P. Landau. 2019. The digitalization of money. Working Paper, National Bureau of Economic Research, September.

Bruno, V., and H. Shin. 2019. Dollar exchange rate as a credit supply factor: evidence from firm-level exports. Report, Bank for International Settlements, November.

Brunton, F. 2019. *Digital Cash: The Unknown History of the Anarchists, Utopians and Technologists Who Created Cryptocurrency*. Princeton University Press.

Buchanan, W., and A. Woodward. 2016. Will quantum computers be the end of public key encryption? *Journal of Cyber Security Technology* 1, 1–22.

Camber, R., and C. Greenwood. 2017. Drug dealers using Bitcoin cashpoints to launder money. *Mail Online*, 4 December (updated). URL: https://dailym.ai/2UkXYyb.

Castillo, M. 2018a. Crypto's top funded startup shutters operations following SEC concerns. *Forbes*, 13 December (updated). URL: http://bit.ly/32nTsRw.

Castillo, M. 2018b. Signature launches institutional payments using permissioned Ethereum blockchain. *Forbes*, 4 December (updated). URL: http://bit.ly/2R6jmoR.

Chadha, J. 2018. Of gold and paper money. Working Paper, Faculty of Economics, University of Cambridge, 2 August.

Chainalysis. 2020. The 2020 state of crypto crime. Report, Chainalysis, January. URL: https://bit.ly/2UabF2C.

Chen, L., S. Jordan, Y.-K. Liu, D. Moody, R. Peralta, R. Perlner and D. Smith-Tone. 2016. Report on post-quantum cryptography. National Institute of Standards and Technology, April.

Chen, Q. 2019. The good, the bad and the ugly of a Chinese state-backed digital currency. *CNBC*, 21 November. URL: https://cnb.cx/2J65mH7.

Coats, W. 2019. Proposal for an IMF Staff Executive Board Paper on promoting market SDRs. *The Bretton Woods Committee*, 19 February. URL: https://bit.ly/3boeRor.

Cœuré, B., and J. Loh. 2018. Bitcoin not the answer to a cash-less society. *Financial Times*, 13 March.

Cohen, B. 2015. *Currency Power: Understanding Monetary Policy*. Princeton University Press.

Cohen, B., and T. Benney. 2014. What does the international currency system really look like? *Review of International Political Economy* 21(5), 1017–1041.

Conway, E. 2014. The Bretton Woods system. In *The Summit: The Battle of the Second World War*, pp. 365–385. London: Little, Brown.

Conway, E. 2019. Facebook currency will help it rule the world. *The Times*, 21 June.

Cooley, J. 2008. *Currency Wars: Forging Money to Break Economics*. London: Constable & Robinson.

Coppola, F. 2019. Libra isn't just a cryptocurrency, it's a threat to national sovereignty. *Wired*, 16 October (updated). URL: http://bit.ly/2RaOZhn.

Dahinden, D., M. Menotti, A. Sprock and A. Verbeck. 2019. Future of money. White Paper, SIX, November.

Davies, R. 2019. *Extreme Economies: Survival, Failure, Future – Lessons from the World's Limits*. London: Bantam Press.

De, N. 2019. In wargaming exercise, a digital yuan neuters US sanctions and North Korea buys nukes. *Yahoo! Finance*, 20 November. URL: https://yhoo.it/33DUg5s.

de Bono, E. 2002. The IBM dollar. In *The Money Changers* (ed. D. Boyle), pp. 168–170. London: Earthscan.

Derby, M. 2019. Powell says Fed has no plans to create digital currency. *Wall Street Journal*, 21 November. URL: https://on.wsj.com/33EAZAU.

DiPrisco, G. 2017. Maker for dummies: a plain English explanation of the Dai stablecoin. *Medium*, 20 November. URL: http://bit.ly/2wEfSCe.

DuPont, Q., and B. Maurer. 2015. Ledgers and law in the block-chain. *King's Review*, 22 June.

Dyson, B. 2019. Can 'stablecoins' be stable? *Bank Underground*, 28 March. URL: http://bit.ly/2SwuY5a.

Dyson, B., and G. Hodgson. 2016. Digital cash: why central banks should start issuing electronic money. Report, Positive Money. URL: https://bit.ly/2xXUXe4.

Dyson, B., and J. Meaning. 2018. Would a central bank digital currency disrupt monetary policy? *Bank Underground*, 30 May. URL: https://bit.ly/2J9R3kF.

E-Commerce in Finance. 2000. Yahoo! offers buyers and sellers person-to-person payment option. *E-Commerce in Finance* 1–2, April.

Economist. 2000. E-Cash 2.0. *The Economist*, 19 February.

Economist. 2017. The Bitcoin bubble. *The Economist*, 1 November. URL: https://econ.st/2UmZjEE.

Economist. 2018. Central banks should consider offering accounts to everyone. *The Economist*, 26 May.

Economist. 2019a. Financial carpet-bombing. *The Economist*, 30 November.

Economist. 2019b. Into the woods. *The Economist*, 17 August.

Economist. 2019c. The rise of the No men. *The Economist*, 4 May.

Economist. 2020. America's aggressive use of sanctions endangers the dollar's reign. *The Economist*, 18 January.

Eichengreen, B. 2019. From commodity to fiat and now to crypto: what does history tell us? Working Paper, National Bureau of Economic Research, January.

Erdbrink, T. 2019. How Bitcoin could help Iran undermine US sanctions. *The New York Times*, 29 January. URL: https://nyti.ms/2UfXPMg.

Essex, D. 1999. Big dreams for tiny money. *Computerworld*, 13 December.

Eyers, J. 2017. ASIC's Greg Medcraft says that traditional bank accounts may be obsolete in a decade. *Australian Financial Review*, 3 September.

FAFT. 2020. Guidance on digital identity. Report, Financial Action Task Force, March.

Farrell, D., and S. Lund. 2000. The end of monetary sovereignty. *The McKinsey Quarterly* **2000**(4), 56–67.

Farrell, H., and A. Newman. 2020. Chained to globalization: why it's too late to decouple. *Foreign Affairs*, January/February.

Ferguson, N. 2001. Understretch: the limits of economic power. In *The Cash Nexus*, pp. 387–416. New York: Allen Lane.

Ferguson, N. 2005. The first 'Eurobonds': the Rothschilds and the financing of the Holy Alliance. In *The Origins of Value: The Financial Innovations that Created Modern Capital Markets* (ed. W. Goetzmann and K. G. Rouwenhorst), pp. 313–326. New York: Oxford University Press.

Ferguson, N. 2012. *The Ascent of Money: A Financial History of the World*. London: Penguin Books.

Ferguson, N. 2017. Networks and hierarchies. In *The Square and the Tower: Networks, Hierarchies and the Struggle for Global Power*, pp. 3–55. London: Allen Lane.

Ferguson, N. 2019. America's power is on a financial knife edge. *The Sunday Times*, 15 September.

Fernández-Villaverde, J., D. Sanches, L. Schilling and H. Uhlig. 2020. Central bank digital currency: central banking for all? Working Paper, National Bureau of Economic Research, January.

Fiedler, S., K.-J. Gern, D. Herle, S. Kooths, U. Stolzenburg and L. Stoppok. 2018. Virtual currencies. Report, European Parliament, June.

Financial Tribune. 2019. Crypto miners can benefit from tax holiday. *Financial Tribune,* 11 September. URL: https://bit.ly/3dqnoTQ.

FinCEN. 2019. Prepared remarks of FinCEN Director Kenneth A. Blanco at Chainalysis Blockchain Symposium. New York: FinCEN.

FINMA. 2018. Guidelines for enquiries regarding the regulatory framework for initial coin offerings (ICOs). Report, Swiss Financial Market Supervisory Authority.

Frankopan, P. 2018. *The roads to the future.* In *The New Silk Roads,* pp. 195–254. London: Bloomsbury.

Gerard, D. 2019. Facebook's new currency has big claims and bad ideas. *Foreign Policy,* 24 June.

Giles, C. 2019. Mark Carney calls for global monetary system to replace the dollar. *Financial Times,* 23 August.

Green, M. 2018. Thirty years of digital currency: from DigiCash to the Blockchain. Speech, Eurocrypt 2018, Tel Aviv, Israel, IACR.

Guttman, R. 2003. *Cybercash: The Coming Era of Electronic Money.* New York: Palgrave Macmillan.

Halton, M. 2019. Why your city should think about starting its own currency. *TED,* 19 July. URL: https://bit.ly/3dsDevN.

Hanke, S., and K. Schuler. 1998. Currency boards and free banking. In *Money and the Nation State* (ed. K. Dowd and R. Timberlake), pp. 403–422. New Brunswick, NJ: Transaction.

Hart, K. 2012. A crisis of money: the demise of national capitalism. *openDemocracy,* 14 March.

Hinge, D. 2019a. Facebook unveils new 'currency'. *Central Banking,* 18 June. URL: https://bit.ly/3dnbmsZ.

Hinge, D. 2019b. New 'currency' aims to tackle failings of its predecessors. *Central Banking,* 10 December. URL: https://bit.ly/33G8geW.

Hockett, R. 2019a. Money's past is fintech's future: wildcat crypto, the digital dollar, and citizen central banking. Article, Cornell Law School, May.

Hockett, R. 2019b. The New York inclusive value ledger: a peer-to-peer savings & payments platform for an all-embracing and dynamic state economy. Research Paper, Digital Fiat Currency Institute, September.

Jeffery, C., and D. Hinge. 2019. Mark Carney on joined-up policy-making, forward guidance and Brexit. *Central Banking*, 19 August.

John, A. 2019. China's digital currency not seeking 'full control' of individuals' details: central bank official. *Reuters*, 20 November. URL: https://reut.rs/3duwltY.

Judson, R. 2017. The death of cash? Not so fast: demand for US currency at home and abroad 1990–2016. Speech, International Cash Conference, Mainau, Germany, Deutsche Bundesbank.

Kajimoto, T., and L. Kihara. 2020. Japan ruling party lawmakers to float idea of issuing digital currency. *Reuters*, 24 January. URL: https://reut.rs/2RliyHe.

Kaminska, I. 2019. Central bank group BIS taps Benoit Cœuré to lead digital currency push. *Financial Times*, 11 November. URL: https://on.ft.com/3dqrOIP.

Kay, J. 2018. Bitcoin: boon or bubble? *John Kay*, 5 March. URL: https://bit.ly/2JedhlM.

Keoun, B. 2019. Top Fed official says US central bank 'actively' debating digital dollar. *Yahoo! Finance*, 16 October. URL: https://yhoo.it/3bl1HBc.

King, J. 2020. China's paytech giants go global. *The Banker*, 2 January.

King, R. 2019. Are we sleepwalking into a cashless society? *Central Banking*, 27 December. URL: http://bit.ly/2QiUObX.

Klein, A. 2020. 70 million people can't afford to wait for their stimulus funds to come in a paper check. *Brookings*, 31 March. URL: https://brook.gs/3dUrP7W.

Knight, W. 2017. China's central bank has begun cautiously testing a digital currency. *MIT Technology Review*, 23 June.

Koning, J. 2016. Thoughts on Rogoff's 'curse of cash'. *Moneyness*, 6 November. URL: http://bit.ly/379haC5.

Koning, J. 2018. Approaches to a central bank digital currency in Brazil. *R3*, 15 October.

Koning, J. 2019. Esperanto, money's interval of certainty, and how this applies to Facebook's Libra. *Moneyness*, 25 June. URL: https://bit.ly/2QH7UQ2.

Kravchenko, P., B. Skriabin and O. Dubinina. 2018. *Blockchain and Decentralized Systems*. Kharkiv, Ukraine: Distributed Lab.

Krupps, M., and H. Murphy. 2019. 'DeFi' movement promises high interest but high risk. *Financial Times*, 29 December. URL: https://on.ft.com/2suqwKm.

Lagarde, C. 2017. Central banking and fintech: a brave new world? Speech, Central Banking and Fintech, London, Bank of England.

Lagarde, C. 2018. Winds of change: the case for new digital currency. Speech, Singapore Fintech Festival, Singapore, MAS.

Lanchester, J. 2019. The invention of money. *The New Yorker*, 29 July. URL: http://bit.ly/2tYR3QD.

Lanier, J. 2013. How will we earn and spend? In *Financial Identity: Who Owns the Future?*, pp. 269–276. London: Allen Lane.

Leng, S. 2019. China appoints new digital currency head as race with Facebook's Libra heats up. *South China Morning Post*, 6 September.

Levin, J., and S. Pannifer. 2015. Demystifying cryptocurrency and the blockchain for the uninitiated. Speech, Cryptocurrency, London, Payments Forward.

Levine, M. 2019. JP Morgan has a coin now. *Bloomberg*, 14 February. URL: https://bloom.bg/2R7yyCh.

Levitin, A. 2014. Bitcoin tax ruling. *Credit Slips*, 26 March. URL: http://bit.ly/2GNnAvR.

Levy, S. 1994. E-money (that's what I want). *Wired*, December.

Libra Association. 2019. An introduction to Libra. Libra Association, 18 June. URL: https://bit.ly/2UN3GaU.

Lonergan, E. 2018. What if your money had a mind of its own? *Prospect*, 17 May, June.

Lowery, C., and V. Ramachandran. 2015. Unintended consequences of anti-money laundering policies for poor countries. Report, Center for Global Development, November.

Lynch, D., and L. Lundquist. 1996. *Digital Money: The New Era of Internet Commerce*. New York: Wiley.

Meyer, C., and M. Hudon. 2018. Money and the commons: an investigation of complementary currencies and their ethical implications. *Journal of Business Ethics* **160**, 277–292.

Michaels, D., and P. Vigna. 2019. The coming currency war: digital money vs. the dollar. *Wall Street Journal*, 22 September.

Nakamoto, S. 2008. Bitcoin: a peer-to-peer electronic cash system. White Paper, Bitcoin.org, 31 October.

Ng, E. 2019. Iran leader urges deeper Muslim links to fight US 'hegemony'. *Associated Press*, 19 December.

NIST. 2016. Quantum-safe cryptography. Report, National Cyber Security Centre, 30 November.

Odlyzko, A. 2011. The collapse of the railway mania, the development of capital markets, and Robert Lucas Nash, a forgotten pioneer of accounting and financial analysis. *Accounting History Review* **21**(3), 309–345.

Orcutt, M. 2020. An elegy for cash: the technology we might never replace. *MIT Technology Review*, 3 January.

Paolo, M. 2019. A brief explainer of mini-BOTS, Italy's parallel currency. *Italics Magazine*, 5 July. URL: https://bit.ly/2UdJMqs.

Pavoni, S. 2020. Sarah Bloom Raskin: the US's focus is misplaced. *The Banker*, 2 January.

Peck, M. 2016. A blockchain currency that beats Bitcoin on privacy. *IEEE Spectrum*, 18 November. URL: http://bit.ly/2UtbjEC.

Petralia, K., T. Philippon, T. Rice and N. Véron. 2019. Banking disrupted? Financial intermediation in an era of transformational technology. Report, International Center for Monetary and Banking Studies, September.

Pilling, D. 2020. A revolution in Africa's relations with France is afoot. *Financial Times*, 1 January. URL: https://on.ft.com/39vF50L.

Popper, N. 2020. Bitcoin has lost steam. But criminals still love it. *The New York Times*, 28 January. URL: https://nyti.ms/37RDO2I.

Pringle, R. 2014. Into the danger zone. In *The Money Trap: Escaping the Grip of Global Finance*, pp. 3–18. London: Palgrave Macmillan.

PYMNTS. 2019. David Marcus threatens that China will win if Libra fails. *PYMNTS*, 17 October. URL: https://bit.ly/2wpvwSw.

Quinn, S., W. Roberds and C. Kahn. 2020. Standing repo facilities, then and now. Research Paper, Federal Reserve Bank of Atlanta, January.

Raskin, M., and D. Yermack. 2016. Preparing for a world without cash. *Wall Street Journal*, 4 August.

Raskin, M., F. Saleh and D. Yermack. 2019. How do private digital currencies affect government policy? Working Paper, SSRN, 14 August.

Ratna, T. 2020. Iran has a Bitcoin strategy to beat Trump. *Foreign Policy*, 24 January. URL: http://bit.ly/2TVad4w.

Rickards, J. 2012. *Currency Wars: The Making of the Next Global Crisis*. New York: Portfolio.

Rogoff, K. 2016. *The Curse of Cash*. Princeton University Press.

Rogoff, K. 2019. The high stakes of the coming digital currency war. *Project Syndicate*, 11 November. URL: https://bit.ly/2wBtb6N.

Sandbu, M. 2020. The dollar is even more dominant than you thought. *Financial Times*, 9 January. URL: https://on.ft.com/33IcvGP.

Schneier, B. 2018. Everyone favours insecurity. In *Click Here to Kill Everybody*, pp. 56–77. New York: Norton.

Scorer, S. 2017. Beyond blockchain: what are the technology requirements for a central bank digital currency? *Bank Underground*, 13 September. URL: https://bit.ly/33IHbb3.

Shuo, W., Z. Jiwei and H. Kan. 2016. Zhuo Xiaochuan interview. *Caxin Online*, 15 February.

Simonite, T. 2013. Mapping the Bitcoin economy could reveal users' identities. *MIT Technology Review*, 5 September. URL: http://bit.ly/3bbcApR.

Son, H. 2019. JP Morgan is rolling out the first US bank-backed cryptocurrency to transform payments business. *CNBC*, 14 February. URL: https://cnb.cx/2uTbqi7.

Stacey, K. 2019. FBI says blockchain expert aided North Korea. *Financial Times*, 30 November. URL: https://on.ft.com/39oXvA9.

Stacey, K., and C. Binham. 2019. Global regulators deal blow to Facebook's Libra currency plan. *Financial Times*, 25 June.

Swanson, T. 2015a. Consensus-as-a-service: a brief report on the emergence of permissioned, distributed ledger systems. *R3 CEV*, 6 April.

Swanson, T. 2015b. Learning from the past to build an improved future of fintech. *Great Wall of Numbers*, 9 July. URL: http://bit.ly/2SmcoM1.

Talley, I., and I. Coles. 2020. US warns Iraq it risks losing access to key bank account if troops told to leave. *Wall Street Journal*, 11 January.

Tenner, T., and S. Utzig. 2019. German banks say: the economy needs a programmable digital euro! *Bankenverband*, 30 October. URL: http://bit.ly/39wvnua.

Tomac, S., and T. Lagodzinski. 2019. Continued evolution in the regulatory framework for virtual currency. *Compass* 6(4), June. Chartwell Partners.

Townsend, E. 2018a. *Beyond Blockchain: The Death of the Dollar and the Rise of Digital Currency.* Independent.

Townsend, E. 2018b. Digital global reserve currency: what would it take? In *The Death of the Dollar and the Rise of Digital Currency*, pp. 187–194. Independent.

Townsend, E. 2018c. Global-scale digital currency. In *The Death of the Dollar and the Rise of Digital Currency*. Independent.

US Department of the Treasury. 2016. Remarks of Secretary Lew on the evolution of sanctions and lessons for the future at the Carnegie Endowment for International Peace. Sanctions and Lessons for the Future. Washington, DC, US Department of the Treasury.

Van Steenis, H. 2019. Future of finance: review on the outlook for the UK financial system. Report, Bank of England, June.

Vigna, P., and Casey, M. 2015. *The Age of Cryptocurrency: How Bitcoin and the Blockchain Are Challenging the Global Economic Order.* New York: St. Martin's Press.

Wang, D. 2020. 2019 letter. *Dan Wang*, 1 January. URL: https://danwang.co/2019-letter/.

Webb, A. 2019. The Rengong Zhineng dynasty: the catastrophic scenario. In *The Big Nine: How the Tech Titans and Their Thinking Machines Could Warp Humanity*, pp. 207–204. New York: Public Affairs.

Werbach, K. 2018. Why blockchain isn't a revolution. *Knowledge@Wharton*, 20 June (retrieved 24 June). URL: https://whr.tn/2WHBqZY.

Wildau, G. 2016. China banks starved of big data as mobile payments rise. *Financial Times*, 29 August.

Wilson, F. 2019. What happened in the 2010s. AVC, 31 December. URL: http://bit.ly/37urX9K.

World Economic Forum. 2020. Central bank digital currency policy-maker toolkit. White Paper, World Economic Forum, Centre for the Fourth Industrial Revolution, January.

You, Y., and K. Rogoff. 2019. Redeemable platform currencies. Working Paper, National Bureau of Economic Research, November.

Zhao, L. 2019. When China and other big countries launch cryptocurrencies, it will kick off a global revolution. *The Conversation*, 12 December. URL: http://bit.ly/2Tnj3rr.

Zhong, S. 2019. China's digital currency debut. *Shanghai Securities News*, 6 September. URL: https://bit.ly/2WR9OSf.

Index